THE VIBRANCY SIGNATURE

*Your Unique Blueprint for
Living Authentically and
with Purpose*

JAMIE CHAMPION

Modern Wisdom Press
Crestone, Colorado, USA
www.ModernWisdomPress.com

Copyright © Jamie Champion 2025

All rights reserved. No part of this publication may be reproduced or transmitted in any form or by any means, mechanical or electronic, including photocopying or recording, or by any information storage and retrieval system, or transmitted by email, without permission in writing from the author. Reviewers may quote brief passages in reviews.

Disclaimer: To protect the privacy of certain individuals, some names and identifying details have been changed. Neither the author nor the publisher assumes any responsibility for errors, omissions, or contrary interpretations of the subject matter within.

Medical Disclaimer: The content in this book is not intended to be a substitute for professional medical advice, diagnosis, or treatment. Always seek the advice of your physician or other qualified health provider for questions you may have regarding a health concern or medical diagnosis.

Published 2025

ISBNs: 978-1-951692-57-5 (paperback)
       978-1-951692-58-2 (eBook)

Cover design by Karen Polaski
Author photos courtesy of Sallie Justice

Advance Praise for The Vibrancy Signature

"Jamie Champion has created a powerful and practical system for understanding who you truly are. *The Vibrancy Signature* is a map to living with vitality, purpose, and authentic self-expression. It blends ancient wisdom with modern energetic science, giving us a new language for our soul's blueprint."

— **Victoria Song**
Wall Street Journal best-selling author of *Bending Reality*

"I love Jamie Champion's astonishing insight into people's strengths and abilities; he has gently guided me into deeper authenticity, aliveness, and relaxed joy. To be accurately seen not only feels fabulous, it also strengthens my physical and psychological resilience and helps me accept myself, love other beings, and enjoy life enthusiastically. Now, for the first time, *The Vibrancy Signature: Your Unique Blueprint* brings Jamie's transformational healing system to the world!"

— **Nancy Manahan, PhD**
Coauthor of *Living Consciously,
Dying Gracefully: A Journey with Cancer and Beyond*

"Jamie Champion has created a framework that's both inspiring and practical. *The Vibrancy Signature* helped me see my own patterns more clearly and gave me tools I can actually use to live and lead with more alignment and purpose. As someone who loves building systems and connecting people to their potential, I found this framework both empowering and immediately applicable in my daily life and relationships. In the book, he offers a clear, structured way to understand your own wiring and live in alignment with it. It's rare to find a book that bridges vision and practicality so well."

— **Oliver Homberg**
CEO, Boston Microgreens
Regenerative Agriculture Leader

"*The Vibrancy Signature* outlines and explains who we are—our unique skills and qualities—and why things happen and recur in our lives. It's a very effective approach that teaches us how we can change and live fuller, more rewarding lives. My work with Jamie has made me much more aware of myself and others. This has been life-changing for me and the loved ones in my life."

— **Jeff Singer**
President and CEO, Electronic Precepts
Marathoner, Fitness Enthusiast, Alternative
Medicine and Natural Healing advocate

"As a client of the Vibrancy Path for over a decade, I can honestly say that Jamie Champion has created a wellness program that is a game-changer for anyone who is seeking a truly holistic approach to their health. This book can be your first step toward a new understanding of who you are and how to become the best version of yourself. The key to unlocking your unique gifts is here. Find your favorite chair and a cozy blanket, and dive in. *The Vibrancy Signat*ure will open a new door to the adventure of being you."

— **Johannah M. Dottori**
Yoga Therapist, RYT500 Yoga Teacher

"Unlock your own transformation with *The Vibrancy Signature*! Jamie Champion's guidance has helped me overcome heart challenges and has allowed me to see who I was born to be. His book holds the wisdom to positively shift your life—a blessing not only to you but also to the world. Please read it, take it to heart, and spread the life-changing message."

— **Bette Sue Wachholz**
Retired, Juice Plus Associate

To the remarkable woman who helped me refine the language of the Vibrancy Signature and continues to inspire me, bringing integrity, compassion, enthusiasm, and beauty into my work and our daily life together.

Chaya, you are the love of my life, my creative partner, and my best friend forever.

Table of Contents

Foreword 9

Introduction 13

PART ONE

Healing and Transforming Your Life
Introducing the Vibrancy Signature & Colorful Vibrancy Powers

Chapter 1 Your Journey to Discovering Your True Self 25

Chapter 2 Fundamentals of the Colorful Vibrancy Powers 35

Chapter 3 The Colorful Vibrancy Powers at a Glance 43

Chapter 4 Understanding the Darkness Before
You Step into the Light 49

PART TWO

Honoring Your Unique, Colorful Nature
The Five Primary Powers of Your Vibrancy Signature

Chapter 5 Your Environment Power:
The First Aspect of Your Vibrancy Signature 61

Chapter 6	Your Expression Power:	
	The Second Aspect of Your Vibrancy Signature.........73	
Chapter 7	Your Intimacy Power:	
	The Third Aspect of Your Vibrancy Signature 83	
Chapter 8	Your Life Force Power:	
	The Fourth Aspect of Your Vibrancy Signature 95	
Chapter 9	Your Intention Power:	
	The Fifth Aspect of Your Vibrancy Signature...........109	

PART THREE

Opening up to a Colorful Future

What's Possible After Discovering Your Vibrancy Signature

Chapter 10	Healing from the Inside Out...................................125	
Chapter 11	Building Bridges to Others 135	
Chapter 12	Your Inner Vibrancy Signature:	
	Take Yourself to the Next Level...............................147	

About the Author *153*

Glossary..*155*

Appendix I: The Complete List of 52 Powers........................... *159*

Acknowledgments *169*

FOREWORD

In 1987, I was in the middle of my residency training in internal medicine when an attending physician named Bill Manahan, MD, took me aside and said:

> Kathryn, what we are teaching you here—physical exams, testing, chemistry, physiology, microbiology, pharmacology—all the ways we understand how to evaluate and treat our patients, will not be the only way we treat illness in 100 years. The future of medicine is **energy**—understanding it and learning how to work with it.

Bill's words intrigued me, but only for a moment, because I had to race off to take care of a critically ill patient. I barely gave any more thought to what he said. After graduating, I devoted the next 20 years to being an internal medicine doctor, practicing primary care at Massachusetts General Hospital and teaching at Harvard Medical School.

While I diligently cared for my patients using conventional medicine skills, I soon discovered that, to my surprise, they were doing things that had not been taught in my medical training.

Curious about why they were seeking care outside the conventional system, I embarked on a journey of exploration.

True to Bill's prescient comments, much of what I discovered involved practitioners with expertise in energy practices such as acupuncture, Jin Shin Jyutsu, qigong, tai chi, and whole-food, plant-based nutrition. I felt surges of excitement whenever I investigated, and I became convinced of the validity of what I was learning.

Slowly but surely, I expanded my offerings by adding new skills and options for myself, my family, and my patients. I describe this holistic way of approaching health and healing as Integrative Whole Health.

In 2010, Bill Manahan introduced me to Jamie Champion and *The Vibrancy Path*. In the years since, my husband David and I have benefited from working with Jamie, as have many patients I have referred to him.

I have loved learning about Jamie's extraordinary, insightful, and groundbreaking work. By exploring our Vibrancy Signatures and by understanding our healthy characteristics and our shadow characteristics, David and I made choices that improved our marriage immensely and inspired us to leave our Boston jobs, move to Europe, and work together to create International Integrators and Living Whole Online, which are creative pursuits that give us purpose.

I hope this book inspires you to join the many others who have discovered their unique Vibrancy Signatures. These 14 special Colorful Powers will help you understand yourself on a much deeper level—an opportunity to explore a lifelong adventure of growth, healing, and joy.

Foreword

Just as the single, colorful fingerprint on the book's cover suggests, your Vibrancy Signature is your unique blueprint. Jamie invites you to truly believe his powerful message: *You are special; there has never been anyone with your unique energetic composition.* Your Vibrancy Signature can help you discover new aspects of yourself and unlock exciting possibilities and purpose.

Whatever life challenges you face, understanding your energetic architecture through your Vibrancy Signature and learning to cherish yourself from this perspective invites you to make the most of your unique talents and live your life aligned with who you truly are.

In working with our Vibrancy Signatures, David and I have learned why we were drawn to each other and to our professions: law and business for David and medicine for me. We gained insight into why we parented our children as we have. We understand more about our relationships with our families of origin. We see what worked well for us and what caused pain, fear, and hardship.

My Power of Prevention (Sea Blue) inspires me to help people with wellness and lifestyle healing, and my Power of Sharing (Peach) motivates me to create and share healing resources with others. David's Power of Leadership (Nectarine) provides professionalism and timely support, and his Power of Inspiration (Apricot) weaves in creative perceptiveness. The Power of Compassion (White) is a color in both of our Signatures, one of the driving talents we are committed to living in our personal lives for ourselves and for all beings. Understanding our Colorful Powers has enabled us to fulfill our desire to offer resources to those also on conscious healing journeys.

We are extraordinarily grateful to Jamie for writing this book as a detailed introduction to the Vibrancy Path. He has infused it with his Power of Hope (Violet), which brings uplift to our needy world. Even better, you will not have to wait the 100 years that Dr. Bill Manahan predicted to experience the transformative power of healing with energy.

— Kathryn Hayward, MD

INTRODUCTION

Let's start this journey together with an undeniable truth: You deserve to live a vibrant life. Indeed, vibrancy is your birthright!

For the many thousands of people I've helped over my 40-plus-year career, living a vitality-filled life seemed out of reach.

You might feel that way too. Imagine having a tool that can precisely map your personality strengths and provide a personalized healing path that pinpoints how to resolve any life stress pattern. Wouldn't you jump at the chance to realize your true potential, while at the same time finding your inner vitality?

The good news is, you are holding that tool in your hands right now. If you are committed to personal growth and self-healing, your Vibrancy Signature is a proven path to inner personal realization, awakening, and transformation. It is based on the understanding that every person has a one-of-a-kind nature that, when embraced, provides congruence and sustained happiness. I have supported people from all over the world who have expressed a desire to find a clear way like this to discover their inner truths.

More good news: No matter how old you are, it's never too late to lead a vibrant, illuminated life. You are gifted with unique powers and sensitivities that have always been your strengths to draw on once you fully realize your own potential.

Step into the Light

It's time for humanity to step into its energetic age once and for all. We need to see ourselves as the multidimensional beings that we truly are. Every person deserves to be treated and valued as a conscious human being, radiating their unique light into the world. This statement is not metaphorical but *literal*.

We are created from the light and sound that form the foundation of every particle in manifestation. Every one of our thoughts, feelings, and inner experiences vibrates inside and all around us. We left the mechanical view of reality behind in 1905 with Einstein's paradigm-shifting view of the universe: $E = mc^2$.

So isn't it about time to start living from this energetic viewpoint instead of merely a chemical, biological, and structural understanding of our human reality?

Let's explore this relatively new worldview, which is based on vibration, energy, and the light of our own consciousness. It's challenging to think of our body as 99.99% empty vibratory space. Yet that's how physics views who we are inside. Unfortunately, in our current and more accepted worldview, chemistry has won out over physics, which is why every answer to our health concerns is primarily pharmacological and not rooted in attuning to our own life balance and inner energetic harmony. As we continue to awaken to our humanity, we'll realize that our inner energetic world is vastly more expansive than just our physical perspective. We can easily change our physiology, metabolism, and psyche when we grasp the principles of our energetic makeup.

One of the main purposes of this book is to help you discover the colorful expressions and vibratory dynamics of your humanity. I call these your "Vibrancy Powers," and sometimes refer to them as your Superpowers to reflect that these ways of being are infused within you, radiating through your physical being and out into the world as your literal contribution to life. By unlocking this code, which is unique to you, you'll have the keys to make informed choices about all aspects of your life that impact your health and wellbeing. These include where and how to live, how to identify and embrace your true calling, how to love and be loved, and how to optimize your wellbeing by leading a mission-driven, intentional life.

My Journey to Vibrancy

Unlike other transformational and healing modalities, the Vibrancy Path offers a fully personalized approach to discovering your soul's purpose, connecting to your innate Power, living with radiant health, and becoming the best version of yourself. Grounded in science and proven effective for thousands of individuals I've helped over the past 40-plus years, your Vibrancy Signature serves as an owner's manual specifically designed for you and your unique physical and psychological makeup. It is the foundation to our journey together on the Vibrancy Path.

The Backstory

My current understanding of our internal vibratory makeup and the principles of personal growth and inner healing reflects a lifetime of researching the deeper reasons for human suffering. At 12, I read *The Making of a Surgeon* by William A. Nolen, MD, and was sure that surgery would be my life path. I imagined myself as a "singing doctor," bopping up and down the halls of a hospital and cheering up my patients with a song just for them. My deeper motivation stems from my experience as a 2-year-old when my father died from a brain tumor, and at age 10, when my mom almost died of a massive heart attack. These two events were deeply traumatic, especially at such a young age, and I've spent many years clearing the emotional scars from that period of time.

Over the years that followed, my healing journey was impacted and sometimes sidetracked by personal grief, addictive coping habits like getting high, and otherwise doing my best to tune out abusive behaviors and emotional pain. On a more positive note, I also found solace in singing, performing, and using my creative imagination. As a teen, I wavered between wanting to be a performer and pursuing a career in medicine. Eventually, I had a lightbulb moment and realized I needed to learn to discover and play my own part in life, starting with serving as an orderly in a community hospital at age 17. There, I followed both of my heart's desires, cheering up patients and closely observing surgeries.

My dream trajectory of becoming a surgeon took a detour during my sophomore year in premed at the University of Michigan. My "Western versus Non-Western Medicine" class exposed me to Ayurvedic and Chinese medicine, hermetic philosophy, Egyptian healing, herbal and nutritional therapies, naturopathic cures, osteopathic manipulation, homeopathic remedies, subtle energetic healing, and chiropractic care.

My favorite subject of all was polarity therapy, developed by Dr. Randolph Stone and taught to me by my mentor Dr. Pierre Pannetier, who advanced Dr. Stone's work. This amazing course investigated belief systems, methods, and the deeper scientific and metaphysical understandings of varied healing modalities. My decision became clear: I wanted to deeply understand and experience the benefits of healing in general, being open to any effective method that was available.

One of the most significant aspects of my education and early professional career was learning the difference between scientific theories and practical experience. My most valuable learning moments came through mentorships and independent studies rather than textbooks. One of my favorite mentors, Ki, was an American Indian medicine woman pursuing her PhD in botany, as her native community no longer believed in or trusted her without a "proper" education. She taught me a great deal about healing and how to use plants as medicine. Each of my mentors shared one common perspective: They viewed the physical body as merely the cover for the emotional, mental, and spiritual core of our humanity.

Creating Vibrancy

My roadmap to discovering the Vibrancy Signature began when I trained in and became certified to practice polarity therapy. Dr. Stone identified the "wireless anatomy" of the human body, mapping out the specific vibrational patterns that exist within it. As a registered Polarity Practitioner, I've been trained to identify where energy and circulation become blocked, as well as which exercises, hands-on therapies, and mindsets can promote renewed balance. Thus, the polarity system approach and Dr. Stone's research laid the foundation for the Vibrancy Signature, which you will explore in depth throughout this book. For now, consider your Vibrancy Signature a blueprint for understanding the intricacies that make you unique and special.

Embracing a New Energetic Paradigm

My career as a professional healer began as a nutritionist. I have always considered healthy eating to be the foundation for good personal health. Good personal health provides energy and clarity to our minds, ultimately supporting our human and spiritual evolution. As the concept of the Vibrancy Signature was taking shape, it became clear to me how much this tool could serve as a powerful personalized guide to nutritional, psychological, and educational health and vitality for others.

Ten years after receiving my degree in human nutritional science, I presented my work at a professional medical symposium in New Delhi, India. Having just received an honorary doctorate in energetic medicine for the Vibrancy Signature, I was speaking on how the soul enters the body and takes physical form. During the talk, the participants tilted their heads from side to side, which I didn't fully understand at the time. It turned out that these highly educated, experienced health professionals and dignitaries validated my research and discoveries of the previous decade, which gave me a deep boost of support and faith. I felt I was on the right path with a modality that reached beyond ethnic, cultural, and scientific boundaries.

My discovery was not based on new information. It was simply that I found a streamlined and practical way to retell the stories of ancient understandings that were grounded in contemporary physics, quantum theory, and holographic science.

One simple illustration can give you a sense of this energetic paradigm we live in regarding medicine and healing. The caduceus is an ancient hermetic medical symbol that represents the human body. Hermes was the Greek messenger of the gods, embodying the peace between Heaven and Earth. The wings of the symbol signify the consciousness and spirit of our humanity. The two intertwining serpents represent the masculine and feminine principles, crossing at each endocrine chakra along the staff, which symbolizes our spinal column.

In contrast, one of the common medical symbols used today lacks the female receptive and nurturing serpent, along with the wings that embody our consciousness and spirit.

How are we truly seen or treated in today's healthcare if we remove these aspects of our humanity? This is why we need to reconnect with the holistic perspective of our true inner nature.

In this book, you will learn about a new language that describes the essential components of the Vibrancy Signature, which encompasses the full spectrum of human attributes and gifts. As you fully embrace and embody your Vibrancy Signature, you embark on a transformative journey. Life's ups and downs can be more easily understood in the context of this new "light-filled" paradigm you're living in as you walk your own unique Vibrancy Path.

How This Book Is Organized

I have designed this book to reflect how you would experience your first introduction to your Vibrancy Signature once an evaluation has been completed by a certified Vibrancy Signature practitioner. By the time you finish reading it, you'll understand how the Vibrancy Signature (and indeed, the entire Vibrancy Path) broadens your perspective on humanity from merely a physical, biological machine formed from random DNA into a unique, divine soul and energetic being that resonates with various patterns of light and sound.

First, I'll lay the groundwork for you by teaching you about the Vibrancy Powers—the 52 beautiful, colorful symphony of light frequencies that live inside of you, just as they live in every human being. I will describe how some of these Powers come together in a very specific way within you, as your Vibrancy Signature, defining how you are literally wired to be, express, and show up in the world. When you are aware of their characteristics and needs, you have immediate access to your own life path and a full understanding of every relationship in your life. This is why my clients who have children say it's the best tool for parenting and understanding their kids. Once couples I've supported learn each other's Vibrancy Signatures, they stop making fun of each other in subtly critical ways and begin to understand, appreciate, and respect each other's differences. And my clients who are business professionals

Introduction

find more creative, productive, rewarding, and profitable ways to exercise their talents.

Next, we will closely examine the five aspects of your Vibrancy Signature—environment, expression, intimacy, life force, and intention—that influence your natural talents and elemental rhythm. It can be challenging to fully embrace your "colorful" gifts that you don't understand or that are out of balance in these five areas, so there is a dedicated chapter for each of these components of your Vibrancy Signature.

There is much more to your fully expressed Vibrancy Signature—you have a lot happening inside energetically! In addition to these five Primary Vibrancy Signature Powers, which define how you show up and express yourself in the world, you also possess nine more Vibrancy Powers that define how you stay emotionally grounded, communicate more effectively, and think clearly. I distinguish these two as your Primary Vibrancy Signature and your Inner Vibrancy Signature.

For this introductory book, I have focused only on the Primary Vibrancy Signature, since it is the most fundamental and is the first step to take on the Vibrancy Path. However, at the end of this book, I will offer a brief overview of the Inner Vibrancy Signature and what it means to have a total of 14 distinct facets to your unique personality. It's a very clear and mathematically compelling approach to truly understanding how you are one of a kind. Once, I calculated the number of possible combinations of Powers, aspects, and traits in the full Vibrancy Signature, and I found over eight quintillion combinations! This is why we say you're entirely original, and no one has ever had the exact same Vibrancy Signature with the same life assignment as you.

PART ONE

Healing and Transforming Your Life

Introducing the Vibrancy Signature & Colorful Vibrancy Powers

CHAPTER 1

Your Journey to Discovering Your True Self

Have you ever wondered why, after years of struggle, you can't seem to get any relief from your personal dilemmas? It may be that you're having a health challenge and have consulted experts, but they don't have the full answer. You might feel confused about what's wrong or out of sync, frustrated that you're not seeing results or feeling better, or even that you're "broken." It could also be that you simply don't feel satisfied with what you're accomplishing or manifesting in your life, sensing that there's more you could or should be doing.

You are not alone. It is common to bounce off the stresses and tensions that surround you and not understand how to address your own struggles. For example, if you tend to be emotionally empathic but don't fully realize it, you'll feel other people's struggles and think they are your problems to solve! This happens more frequently than you might imagine.

Throughout my career helping thousands of people resolve "unsolvable" problems, I have learned that there is a unique path for each person to follow for their optimal health and vitality—and the best part is that you were born with the blueprint to uncover that within your very own cells. This is your Vibrancy Signature, a powerful tool that helps you recognize your sensitivities, personality traits, and specific needs, as well as understand how they impact your balance and wellbeing. Once you are aware of your inherent gifts, navigating your daily experiences becomes much easier, allowing you to avoid being lost, sidetracked, and enmeshed in the concerns or problems of others.

Learning to Walk

What leads to suffering begins in early childhood. Consider this: How much of what you needed to thrive did you receive? Were you validated, encouraged, and supported for your uniqueness? Or did the education and other early messages you received confine you to stereotypes and judgments about how smart or capable you are? Maybe you heard that you didn't measure up in class. Did you fight back, rebel, sink into depression, or become the class clown and pretend not to care about what others think? You may have employed these or other coping methods to deal with external judgment—perhaps you still use these strategies today. However, their ignorance and lack of understanding did not have to become your source of suffering or self-condemnation.

Imagine how different it could have been if your parents, teachers, and other guiding figures in your young life had truly understood you. It would have made a big difference, wouldn't it? Your self-esteem, confidence, and self-awareness would have instantly kept you from sliding into distraction or distress. You would have focused on finding inspiring ways to live authentically and express your energetic self. I estimate that 9 out of 10 of my clients experience major personality distress that traces back to those early years.

This is where knowing your Vibrancy Signature, which begins at birth and has its core facets cemented within you by your first birthday, could have made all the difference in how successfully you channeled your natural gifts.

You're Born a Superhero—You Just Needed to Know Your Powers!

Many years ago, I had the good fortune to receive a grant to implement a Kinder Colors program for a small group of five-year-olds and their parents. Imagine yourself in kindergarten, discovering your five special superpowers and playing with the kids in your class using your natural gifts.

My favorite memory is about a little boy who was often teased by the other kids in his class for giving his mom lingering hugs when she dropped him off at school. Knowing that he had the Vibrancy Power of Love with the Vibrancy Color of Pink in his Vibrancy Signature (more on Vibrancy Powers and Colors in Chapter 2), I dubbed him Super Hugger. From that moment on, he felt validated and encouraged, allowing him to stand up to the bullies. He told the kids "Of course I'm going to hug my mom; I'm a Super Hugger." This extremely sensitive and openhearted little boy was now able to see his emotional tenderness as a gift and not something to shut down or be embarrassed by.

What would it have felt like to be recognized for your superpowers at such a formative and tender age?

Are you ready to join those who have learned how to heal themselves from these unsupportive messages seeded in the past? The answer lies in understanding and aligning with your natural way of being and not reacting to what others have said or judged. Without that, without challenging and overcoming these painful messages, an internal struggle develops between the part of you that knows deep down that you are special and the part that fights against being labeled in a cruel and often unconscious manner. The most common, but limiting, response to this is to hide from or push against others who perpetuate these beliefs.

It's not always easy to revisit wounds, humiliation, or abuse. However, from my experience, with the right kind of support, the body quickly releases trauma when the narrative is completely reframed with a new healing and empowered inner dialogue. Your body and mind are not trapped by these early unconscious stresses or trauma patterns; you simply have not yet found the key to unlock them.

When those old narratives are replaced with new ones that reflect your true value and your way of being and showing up in the world, you can learn to appreciate, validate, and advocate for yourself in ways you never were able to before. Once you know your Vibrancy Signature, you'll be able to give yourself the guidance you have always wanted to receive. You will understand how to comfort yourself in ways that help you relax, unwind, and discover a genuine inner sense of ease. You can start fresh, let go of what others taught you about yourself, and renew your educational credentials, so to speak—not according to what you were told, criticized for, or rewarded for, but with your stamp of approval and loving acceptance.

The Vibrancy Signature: Your Unique Owner's Manual

When you're lost and trying to follow someone else's suggestions or directions, you'll typically feel bored, frustrated, dissatisfied, and a bit hopeless. You may be frightened that you're never going to be healthy and resolve your inner suffering. Perhaps you're trying to discover how to energize your sense of purpose and find your true life calling. All these puzzles in your life connect to the same root cause. You have a particular personality with specific needs, desires, and goals that you may not be fully embracing.

Your happiness and vitality depend on being aligned with your true self. Every health struggle, career setback, relationship rift, and personal pain stems from not living true to your unique Vibrancy Signature.

If you're like most people, you probably know more about your home appliances, your bank account, and your children's school activities than you do about your daily personality needs. Relying on simplistic and partially accurate personality categories is insufficient for recognizing your full uniqueness and innate capability. When you understand your natural gifts and true Powers, you'll

> **Every health struggle, career setback, relationship rift, and personal pain stems from not living true to your unique Vibrancy Signature.**

start getting the answers you've been looking for in your life. Since 1981, I have never had a client who didn't see themselves in a new and clearer light after discovering their own Vibrancy Signature—their true inner wiring.

Your Vibrancy Signature is the unique description of the light frequencies reflected in your humanity from the source of your soul spark. When you get to know your Vibrancy Signature—something a certified practitioner is trained to identify—you can begin to imagine a world where you not only understand yourself better but also find ways to support and love others more effectively.

March to the Beat of Your Own Drum

The most important thing to remember is that you're perfectly fine just the way you are. You're not a particular pathology or any other negative label. You may have weaknesses, insecurities, and self-doubts, just like everyone else, but none of that defines who you are. As you uncover who you truly are, you'll learn that not only can you march to the beat of your own drum, but as a unique individual, that's the only way to roll.

There are five primary aspects of your Vibrancy Signature. They define your natural gifts, your ideal tempo, and the many unique facets of your nature that make your life enjoyable and interesting, allowing you to ultimately be yourself. Achieving psychological and physiological balance in life requires knowing how to work with these aspects of yourself, enabling you to effortlessly access your innate talents.

Below is a summary of the information that is energetically "written" in your Vibrancy Signature. As you will learn, we use the language of Vibrancy Powers to define these gifts that you embody.

- Your **Environment Power** reflects the rhythm of your nervous system and the best way you can find relaxation and ease in your life.

- Your **Expression Power** helps you determine the most suitable career and hobbies, which will rejuvenate you and provide a sense of inner satisfaction.

- Your **Intimacy Power** empowers you to cultivate strong connections with friends and family, even when engaging in your solo recharge activities.

- Your **Life Force Power** illuminates the rhythm of your life, engaging your senses to create a day filled with passion and energy.

- Your **Intention Power** gives you a "theme song" in life, one that plays a particular rhythm and weaves through everything you do.

Keep in mind that these five aspects of your Vibrancy Signature will not change in your lifetime. What does change is how you learn to adapt and harness these Powers and gifts that they reveal as yours to give. Think of it as receiving five different instruments to master and then spending a lifetime practicing and playing this special music of your personality. You'll learn to create your own unique harmony and use your ingenuity to shape your multifaceted personality dynamics.

When you recognize and understand each of your Vibrancy Powers and learn how to keep each of them in balance, they cooperate, complement, and collaborate with one another, allowing you to experience deep self-love and live your life fully. And then you can begin to discover your true self.

The Holographic Energy of Your Vibrancy Signature

As you deepen your understanding of each of your five Primary Vibrancy Powers, I will connect them to specific parts of your holographic energy body, as identified in polarity therapy by Dr. Randolph Stone.

A hologram is simply a three-dimensional image broadcast by a laser light. In your case, the laser light is the light of your soul transmitted through your specific Vibrancy Signature. Think of this as the energetic blueprint that holds your cells together. Each of these aspects is an energetic pattern that comprises your Vibrancy Signature.

Evaluating Your Vibrancy Signature

A Vibrancy Signature evaluation, provided by a certified practitioner, lasts a lifetime. Your Vibrancy Powers never change, but rather, like a fine wine, they get more developed, mature, and distinctive over time. Just as the many facets of the human body mature and evolve, each of your Vibrancy Power gifts and talents also grows with each passing year and phase of life. Like a cultured scholar, brilliant inventor, skilled painter, or any other unique talent, these parts of your personal Vibrancy Signature makeup are honed and refined throughout your life, always bringing their characteristic voice, beauty, and contribution to your life and, through you, into the world.

Your Vibrancy Signature arises from the energetic blueprint patterns woven from your DNA inheritance.

My polarity therapy mentor gave me the physiological understanding of the "wireless anatomy" that exists within the human body. From there, I uncovered the 52 Vibrancy Powers and eventually developed a technique for resonating with each of them as they vibrated throughout the body. Over the years, I have utilized an energetic pulse evaluation on specific points that resonate with the Vibrancy Powers in each aspect of a person's Vibrancy Signature. I have also worked with client DNA samples of hair, teeth, saliva, and sweat. This is just the beginning of this energetic field of study. I believe that given the current speed and depth of technological advances, this process of evaluating human and animal Vibrancy Signatures will only become easier and more efficient over time.

> **Your Vibrancy Signature arises from the energetic blueprint patterns woven from your DNA inheritance.**

To join the most successful and happy people in the world, you must be willing to seek support when you need it. It isn't a sign of weakness to ask for help; it's a sign of your internal strength and your willingness to be vulnerable, brave, and honest. Even though the growth process of reclaiming your sense of self-worth and vibrancy may take you to unfamiliar places, the Vibrancy Signature is 100% life-affirming and supports you in living the life you've always been meant to live with minimal negative side effects.

CHAPTER 2

Fundamentals of the Colorful Vibrancy Powers

There is a language being spoken within you that helps spell out the many facets of your humanity. This is the language of your Vibrancy Signature, which shows you how to engage in your life to reap the benefits of vital health, better relationships, and soul fulfillment. I am inspired to help you gain fluency in this language. Learning it will help you understand yourself and others better, and it will help you solve almost any problem, confusion, or personal dilemma you may have.

This language is made up of the 52 Vibrancy Powers, and each is associated with a particular frequency of light, or Vibrancy Color, five of which make up your Primary Vibrancy Signature. This is why I often refer to them as "Colorful Vibrancy Powers." As you begin to explore the fundamental principles of these Colorful

Vibrancy Powers, think of them as an alphabet representing the full range of your human attributes and needs that impact your physiological functions and psychological insights.

When you live in balance and harmony with them, you achieve a natural equilibrium. You resonate with "the light side" or the balanced nature of these Vibrancy Powers vibrating within you. However, when you disconnect from this inner light, shadows such as distortion, depression, disease, and disharmony may arise.

You always have the choice to either embrace your gifts or deny and stuff them away. You also have the right to discover and actualize your true, healthiest light and not be misled by shadow patterns or wounds that may temporarily surface. You can live your life knowing that it's possible to overcome struggles once you understand the Vibrancy Power issue that's involved and what it needs to return to homeostasis.

The Rainbow Connection

Every human being is a collection of light energies: the 52 Vibrancy Powers. These energies can be categorized by color. However, your expression of individual vibrancy is unique (your Vibrancy Signature). You can grasp this concept of light energies by considering something colorful that captivates us all: a rainbow.

Do you know how a rainbow is created? It all starts with the sun, which appears to be white light. But it's actually composed of all the different colors the human eye can see (red, orange, yellow, green, blue, indigo, violet). These visible colors each have unique characteristics or wavelengths.

Through air, light moves very quickly—literally at the speed of light. But when it moves through denser mediums such as water, it slows down and bends. So when light enters a water droplet after a storm, it reflects off the inside of the droplet, separating into its component wavelengths—or colors. When it exits the droplet, that light scatters or refracts, making a rainbow. And as you might imagine, no two rainbows are the same. You are like a rainbow in that way.

The essential way light is reflected in your system—which is established in your first year of life—informs how you can shimmer and shine in the most stunning, vibrant way possible.

> The essential way light is reflected in your system—which is established in your first year of life—informs how you can shimmer and shine in the most stunning, vibrant way possible.

How I Discovered the 52 Colors and Their Vibrancy Powers

My journey to discovering this amazing language of humanity began during my fascination with physics and energetic healing modalities. Always drawn to insightful, cutting-edge thinking and healing discoveries, I came across the research of Dr. Barbara Bowers, a psychologist and clairvoyant who correlated specific auric patterns (light frequencies around the body) with distinct personality types. Her book *What Color Is Your Aura?* brought me to a pivotal moment in my own healing explorations. Naturally, I wanted to know my personal aura color. After studying the book, I guessed my first color was indigo light, which she described as having a strong intuitive nature. Later, I learned from a friend that the author was expanding her color list, prompting me to explore my own theory about the total number of additional colors that exist.

After extensive soul-searching and research, I found that a total of 52 colors resonate within the human body—each linked to a specific Power or characteristic capability—consolidating my previous 10 years of study. Here's a quick overview of the significant correlations that informed the development of the 52 Vibrancy Powers array.

- Ayurvedic medicine directly connects to Sanskrit, the world's oldest alphabet, which has 52 letters that also correspond to beautiful, vocal, resonant mantra sounds.

- The Chinese system of meridians could also be correlated with these same harmonic patterns.

- Dr. Stone's Polarity Therapy Books, of which there are many, map out the energetic patterns of the body. I discovered that these energy patterns are each vibrating at a distinct light harmonic, which is the colorful (light) Vibrancy Powers.

- Every week of the year is a new reminder of one of the internal Colorful Vibrancy Powers that resonates inside you. Each of these 52 Colorful Vibrancy Powers is either in tune or out of its natural vibratory balance.

I then uncovered the physiological and psychological distinctions of each of these 52 light-frequency patterns. Each Vibrancy Power has a unique descriptive name and a colorful light-frequency name associated with it as well.

Discovering the 52 Vibrancy Powers was for me like finding the Rosetta Stone, which allowed researchers to translate Egyptian hieroglyphic writing for the first time. Similarly, by understanding the energy language that lives inside us, I realized that I could translate any modern or ancient healing discipline or system that I'd previously studied.

The Vibrancy Powers and the Healing Possibilities

What you're thinking, feeling, or struggling with can be systematically correlated to specific Vibrancy Powers within you that need support and balancing.

Any problem, worry, or concern connects with an imbalance in one of your Vibrancy Powers.

When I identified and categorized these 52 Powers, I realized that a whole new level of holistically effective healing was possible.

> Any problem, worry, or concern connects with an imbalance in one of your Vibrancy Powers.

Your body is constantly communicating with you, letting you know what it needs and how it feels. And if you know that any discomfort, tension, or physical body reaction is directly associated with a particular Vibrancy Power, then you can see why understanding this language can come in handy throughout your lifetime. It will help you understand what your body is truly saying and what it fundamentally needs to achieve balance and harmony.

Each Colorful Vibrancy Power correlates to a specific vibratory harmonic that creates balance and stability in mind and body.

Every therapeutic diet, medical procedure, philosophy, or healing practice attempts to create that same balance. With the discovery of these Powers, I now had an effective way to translate the varied healing perspectives into what the body and psyche specifically needed.

This inspired me to cross-reference natural foods, herbs, flowers, gems, and a whole host of other natural and chemical medicinal products to determine their corresponding Colorful Vibrancy Powers. Understanding the energetic makeup of the substances we typically nourish ourselves with could be a game-changer when it comes to enhancing our capacity to heal. If you know the Vibrancy Power within you that needs support, it stands to reason that eating foods or taking herbs and supplements with that same vibration will go a long way in fostering your recovery.

I also correlated specific psychological affirmations, behaviors, emotions, and attitudes with the Vibrancy Powers. Similarly, by understanding these kinds of connections, a person can chart a clear path to reclaim their balance across all aspects of their being—physical, emotional, psychological, and even spiritual. I realized that once I knew a person's issue was related to an imbalance of a particular Vibrancy Power, I could provide tailored guidance specifically for that Power's regeneration.

This was the goal of my research—to find ways to facilitate others (and myself) in returning to what is our human birthright: a sense of health, equilibrium, and wellbeing. Today, most of my time is focused on Vibrancy Healing. This is the process I developed that grew out of the discovery of the 52 Vibrancy Powers and how to work with them to identify which imbalanced patterns contribute to the stress and hardship that my clients face and the steps they must take to return them to balance.

Each Vibrancy Power Has a Universal Element

The Vibrancy Powers are not only associated with a particular frequency of light and color, but also with one of five universal elements: earth, water, fire, air, and space (ether in Ayurvedic circles). These elemental types represent the five ancient universal elements from Ayurvedic tradition.

Some Vibrancy Powers vibrate at an earthy pace, providing consistency and grounded foundations for your health and wellbeing. Others are watery Vibrancy Powers, which provide a quality of support, sustenance, and nurturing to every facet of life. Next are Vibrancy Powers which have a fiery nature, giving you drive, energy, and the willingness to keep your life moving forward. Then there are Air Vibrancy Powers, which are known for generating lots of ideas, fresh perspectives, and the speed to keep things moving efficiently. Lastly, there are Space Vibrancy Powers. These generate creative possibilities, expansive new horizons, and the time needed to decompress in solitude.

Each Vibrancy Power has a unique and distinct elemental nature, rhythm, pace, and aptitude. To maintain a balanced life, you must nourish and attend to the unique needs of each Vibrancy Power.

How the Colorful Vibrancy Powers Keep Your Life in Tune

When you start to consciously understand each of the Vibrancy Powers, you are discovering the secrets to keeping your life in harmony, happiness, and success. Every time you feel "out of sorts," defeated, or frustrated, it means you are out of tune with one or more Vibrancy Powers inside you.

Whether consciously or unconsciously, the way you express yourself in life is as though you are playing a piano of human tunes in the form of Vibrancy Powers. Sometimes, your life experience may resemble a cat going up and down the piano keys, and other times, you may feel like you've just composed a beautiful song. When your "music" sounds discordant and full of off notes, you have a life stress going on that is related to an internal wiring of discordant Vibrancy Powers inside you. Once you understand the "musical chord" needed for healing, you can relieve constriction and tension while training your cells to work in harmony.

By knowing and understanding the Vibrancy Powers, you are embracing the full scope of your humanity. This helps you become consciously aware of and resonate with each Colorful Vibrancy Power that is part of your human nature.

CHAPTER 3

The Colorful Vibrancy Powers at a Glance

Understanding the 52 Vibrancy Powers is life-changing. A wise physics teacher of mine, also trained in deep metaphysical principles, once told me that human atomic energy equals the power of 16 suns. So the next time you think you are weak, powerless, or insignificant, think again.

When you hold the perspective of yourself as energetic and filled with light, you won't be inclined to minimize or discount who and what you are.

You deserve to be seen, honored, and given the chance to express

> You deserve to be seen, honored, and given the chance to express and share your unique light and powerful gifts with the world, because that is your true inheritance.

and share your unique light and powerful gifts with the world, because that is your true inheritance.

Before we go any further, let's recap the most fundamental features of the Vibrancy Powers.

- Each Vibrancy Power is comprised of specific light frequencies.

- Each Vibrancy Power has an associated color name.

- Each Vibrancy Power has the potential for either a positive (light) or negative (shadow) trait.

- Every discord in your life (for example, disease, toxicity, stress pattern) has a corresponding dissonance in your body that can be balanced by identifying the Vibrancy Powers that require support.

- Each Vibrancy Power has an elemental nature that predisposes it to a distinct rhythm, pace, and aptitude. These elemental types are the five ancient universal elements of Ayurvedic tradition: earth, water, fire, air, and ether (or space).

The Vibrancy Powers: The Building Blocks of Your Vibrancy Signature

Remember when you were learning the alphabet and discovered that your name is spelled with just some of those letters? It is the same thing with the 52 Vibrancy Power "alphabet"; 14 of the 52 Vibrancy Powers are the building blocks of your unique Vibrancy Signature. And when you're attempting to access your own personal gifts and talents, they take the form of these specific Powers that are hardwired inside you and spell your energetic "name."

The Vibrancy Signature in Action: Learning to Live with Gusto!

Rose had ALS, a condition that allows for sensation but ultimately results in the loss of motor function. While her caregivers meant well by encouraging her to confront her (apparently) grim future, Rose was not placated. In fact, she felt frustrated and horrified that their advice was to embrace what she termed a "dying attitude."

What these caregivers didn't realize was that Rose, a free spirit in her own right, wasn't wired to give up on life. I recognized this immediately when I evaluated her Vibrancy Signature and began working with her. I discovered that she possessed the Vibrancy Power of Authenticity, which correlates with the Vibrancy Color Lavender. She preferred to embody an adventurous and life-exploring perspective throughout her day and to see hope for her future, not just death. She wanted to have rich, authentic connections with every new person she met. Looking at this one aspect of her individuality and Vibrancy Signature, Rose understood that each day she thrived when she followed her heart and pursued what she loved. She sought to enjoy her life, along with the spontaneous conversations and authentic sharing that came naturally to her in every moment, regardless of her circumstances.

Through our work together, Rose came to fully embrace her unique, eclectic way of being and understand that one of the secrets to living life to its fullest was for her to be genuine and true to herself, appreciating each day as a gift. She ended up being a teacher for her hospice caregivers, opening them to a new perspective on the dying process. From Rose's standpoint, her declining motor functions and ultimate death did not need to be solely mournful and sad but could instead be celebratory and lively along the way.

A Taste of the Colorful Powers Possible in Your Vibrancy Signature

The first step is to become familiar with each of your Vibrancy Signature Powers—getting a sense of what it's like to have those specific Powers holding you together. And then learn how to support yourself in living true to these parts of your individuality.

For now, just to give you a taste of the 52 Vibrancy Powers possible in your Vibrancy Signature, here's a sample overview of 10 of them and their healthy qualities. While the examples in the following chart may or may not be part of your Vibrancy Signature, it will give you an idea of what we mean by Colorful Powers.

Sample Overview of 10 Colorful Vibrancy Powers

- **Power of Altruism (Blue Topaz)**: deeply values life, purpose-driven, committed to humanitarian causes, activist

- **Power of Compassion (White)**: communes on a feeling level, emotionally comforting, good listener, empathetic

- **Power of Connecting (Indigo Topaz)**: inclusive, bridge-builder, promotes cooperation, appreciates diversity, diplomatic

- **Power of Hope (Violet)**: idealistic, sees possibilities, offers uplifting perspective, shares visionary ideas

- **Power of Integrity (Red Topaz)**: has high standards, values boundaries and clear agreements, naturally athletic

- **Power of Leadership (Nectarine)**: has natural business savvy, provides structure for success, values timeliness

- **Power of Love (Pink)**: openhearted, gives love easily, gentle, promotes kindness, likes to give hugs

- **Power of Prevention (Sea Blue)**: sensitive, needs to feel safe, proactive, wellness-oriented, safety-minded

- **Power of Relaxation (Mocha)**: unwinds easily, good at simplifying, keeps life uncomplicated, Zen-like creativity

- **Power of Support (Silver)**: service-oriented, volunteer spirit, needs to give and receive support equally

This simple summary of the Vibrancy Powers is only the tip of the iceberg. There are numerous nuances to each Power, with many layers to explore and understand, but this journey unfolds organically over time with increased exposure. You'll find the full list of all the Vibrancy Powers in the appendix at the back of this book. There's no rush to "get it and move on." That's why this is called the Vibrancy Path: It will continue to unfold as you recognize and celebrate the parts of you that you know well—and befriend those you may have left behind, neglected, or maybe never really knew.

After you receive your Vibrancy Signature, you can start by "trying on" these particular energies and noticing what it's like to view yourself in this positive light, observing where you see that gift show up in your life, and getting curious when you aren't so sure it even exists. The next step after anchoring the concepts of your Colorful Vibrancy Powers has to do with where these Powers live within you. Each has a particular role to play and job to do when it comes to you being your authentic self.

In the coming chapters, you'll learn about the five aspects of your Primary Vibrancy Signature in depth. The first three aspects—Environment, Expression, and Intimacy—oversee specific facets of your life. The last two—Life Force and Intention—weave through all aspects of your full Vibrancy Signature. By taking a deep dive into each one, you'll gain a better understanding of how vital, energizing, and fulfilling life can be when your Powers are in balance—and how challenging it is to your health and wellbeing when they are not.

So before we explore the five Primary Vibrancy Powers in depth, we'll take a quick detour into the shadowlands—that place that diminishes your energy and dims or even extinguishes your inner light.

CHAPTER 4

Understanding the Darkness Before You Step into the Light

When you're living in balance and harmony, there is a natural equilibrium within you. You naturally resonate with the light or balanced nature of your internal Vibrancy Powers. However, when you shut yourself off from your inner light, shadows of distortion, depression, disease, and disharmony will arise. As a human being, you're always shifting from shadow to light in a consciousness dance inside your own being. You have the right to discover and reveal your truest, healthiest self, free from the influence of wounded shadow patterns that may temporarily reside within you.

Overview of the Shadow Concept

Any emotionally painful part of your life history is when you were living through the shadowlands of your Vibrancy Signature characters. When I say "shadowlands," I mean your experiences that lacked the light of understanding of who you are, what you need, and how you're nourished each day.

A plant that needs sun will not bloom well in the shade, and neither will you.

> A plant that needs sun will not bloom well in the shade, and neither will you.

The concept behind your Vibrancy Signature gifts and talents implies unique, innate strengths and a natural way of expressing your authentic self, leading to a vibrant and fulfilling life. When you don't embrace your true personality strengths, you often experience a range of "shadow traits" and struggles, as described by psychological concepts like Carl Jung's "shadow self" and the general impact of inauthenticity.

In this chapter, we'll explore some of the most common shadow qualities, and you'll see how knowing your Vibrancy Signature empowers you to step into the light.

Diminished Self-Esteem and Self-Worth

Whenever you live in self-doubt and insecurity, it will eat away at your confidence and can make living in your body a chore of constant discomfort. If you are not in alignment and relaxing into your true strengths, it can make you feel like you're not "enough" or even know who you truly are. This can make you indecisive about where your life is going and leave you feeling unsure, scattered, and confused.

Once you're stuck in a cycle of chronic self-criticism, you may feel that you've lost the joy and fun of being you. Instead of finding creative opportunities to play, dance, and celebrate life, you spend your time tuning in to your internal critic, which constantly points out your perceived flaws and shortcomings. This is why you may find yourself seeking ways to numb this self-inflicted pain. Imagine a performer who is constantly booed or hissed; eventually, they will lose the joy of their own craft. Likewise, you may find yourself turning away from your natural gifts and desires.

Low confidence diminishes your self-respect and makes you question your worth. When you don't express what naturally and powerfully comes from within, your confidence in your abilities and decisions about your life purpose can wane. This leads to a whole host of psychological stress patterns and, in general, can make your life miserable. This is why, when you first avail yourself to your true colorful reflection and see what's there, you begin feeling the warmth of that inner recognition and begin stepping out of the darkness.

Inauthenticity and Dissociation

What mask do you wear regularly? Do you find yourself adopting a certain face that you think will make you popular or help you fit in? Or are you seeking validation and approval from those around you? These days, in an age where "likes" and social status are everything, you might present a persona to the world that isn't your true self, leading to a feeling of disconnection from your feelings and natural desires. Living in this artificial world of inauthenticity and people-pleasing can make you wonder where you've gone. Your strong desire to fit in or gain approval may suppress your unique expression, causing you to forget your own vibrant nature.

This dissociation from your Vibrancy Signature Powers is what causes you to feel lost, sick, and tired. It's always exhausting to be someone you're not wired to be, but embracing who you truly are can be effortless, energizing, and rewarding. Over time, consistently suppressing your authentic self can lead to a pervasive sense of emptiness, as if you lack a distinct personality of your own.

This is why you must give yourself time to let your Vibrancy Signature's natural gifts and beauty sink in and wake up some of the emotional numbing and suppression that might have taken place. You may have had to suppress your true emotions, including joy and passion, to avoid expressing your "unacceptable" vibrant qualities. This can be challenging at times, especially if there are generational "shadow traits" that have been passed down.

Frustration, Resentment, and Unexpressed Energy

Have you ever wondered why you feel frustrated or have internal turmoil for no apparent reason? It's almost always directly related to your unexpressed gifts being pent-up inside you. Your need for fun, creativity, productivity, or simply new experiences might be tugging at you. When you feel stuck or unfulfilled, you have pent-up energy that must be channeled toward one of your many Vibrancy Power gifts inside you that, for whatever reason, doesn't have a healthy outlet yet. This is especially true for you when you have creative talents, manifesting abilities, and leadership inclinations. You need to express that energy rather than bottling it up inside, which leads to frustration.

Whenever you hold on to internal resentments, they may surface when you are around people who are freely expressing similar gifts, or toward yourself for being afraid to courageously share your own talents. For example, if you have inside yourself the Colorful Power of Fun (Yellow), and you have found yourself in the shadow of this Power, instead of using your creative, playful, and fun-loving nature, you find yourself in the "dark" with constant critical thoughts and an all-work-and-no-play attitude. You would be resentful of all the fun you were missing out on that you would truly feel more aligned with expressing. So when you hang out with a fun-loving person, initially you may feel some form of painful triggering response inside yourself. This may show up as passive-aggressive behavior toward those who could ideally be your Vibrancy Power allies, rather than someone who reminds you how miserable you are for not expressing your talents. Your suppressed emotions and desires can surface in indirect or unhealthy ways. Ultimately, they are here to get your attention and wake you up to what's truly important to you.

As you check in with the health status of each of your Colorful Vibrancy Powers, you'll recognize where you stand on the light and prosperous side of the balance sheet, versus the "energetic debt" side, which stems from drained talents that have not been recharged. Whenever you spend energy trying to be someone you're not, it can lead to exhaustion and deplete your natural vitality. When you express your own Vibrancy Powers every day, you naturally recharge and awaken to your true potential. This is both energizing for you and beneficial for the world that gains from your gifts.

Projection, Avoidance, and Self-Sabotage

If someone has ever told you that you are too "sensitive," "bossy," "kind," or any other adjective meant to judge, criticize, or be a backhanded compliment, they are, quite possibly, projecting their own internal wounds onto you. This happens when they are unconsciously out of balance with that Vibrancy Power quality, and so they recoil from it when they notice it expressed in you.

The next time someone believes you have a "too" problem, pause and consider whether their judgment is helpful, or merely a projection of their own pain.

It is possible that the "too" problem is what's called an excessive shadow aspect of a Vibrancy Power, but it's also possible that it's just the other person's projection. To illustrate what I mean, here are three examples of how a Power gets labeled as excessive, and how I might encourage you to not accept that judgment, celebrate your gift, and stand up for yourself in a loving way.

- "Too sensitive" is an excessive shadow issue for the Power of Prevention (Sea Blue). When a person is balanced and healthy with that Power, they are naturally sensitive, proactive, wellness-oriented, and safety-minded. If this is you, instead of allowing someone else to judge you negatively, try inviting them to accept and appreciate you, and possibly heal a wounded piece of themselves, by responding with something like, "The world needs more sensitivity. When you want to create more safety and wellness in your life, I'm your person."

- "Too bossy" is a shadow aspect of the Power of Leadership (Nectarine), which has a natural business savvy, provides structure for success, and values timeliness. If you're confident you aren't in the shadow, turn that projection around by saying "When you need help making a decision, or taking charge of a project, give me a call!"

- "Too kind" is usually just a negative projection from someone out of balance with the Power of Love (Pink), which is openhearted and gentle, gives love easily, and promotes kindness. Own this gift by telling others "Whenever you are in emotional pain, I am here for you with all my heart and willing to give you some hugs and love."

Another example of shadow expression is when you're avoiding a task or a personal goal. You may have a fear of failure or judgment, stemming from not trusting your true abilities. This paralysis is related to insecurity about being yourself. You'll find excuses to avoid the task or goal and even dismiss the importance of this need in your life. Whenever someone in your life didn't recognize your value, importance, or true abilities, it is a painful chapter in your history. The good news is that those moments can now begin to be rewritten with your own self-affirmation and respect. As soon as you begin to own your Vibrancy Signature Powers, inertia and confusion will diminish, and your ability to embrace your goals will become progressively easier. For a comprehensive view of the 52 Colorful Vibrancy Powers, along with their healthy or shadow characteristics, see the appendix at the back of the book.

Finally, you may experience times in your life where you feel stuck in an addictive behavior that you know is not what you want, but you're trapped in a social dilemma. Most likely, you are seeking external validation or turning to coping mechanisms to fill the void left by unexpressed authenticity.

When you hide who you truly are, you prevent genuine emotional intimacy, as authentic connection requires vulnerability and honesty.

This fear of being you can make you gravitate toward relationships where your vibrancy and authenticity are not encouraged or are actively suppressed by your self-sabotaging behavior.

> When you hide who you truly are, you prevent genuine emotional intimacy, as authentic connection requires vulnerability and honesty.

When you find people or a community that gets you for your own Vibrancy Signature nature, the struggle and pain will start to go away. Your personality transformation is possible and can help you to break any bad habit or dysfunctional relationship.

Summary of Living in Your Shadow

Failing to tap into your unique, positive, light-filled Vibrancy Signature and fully recognize your gifts, talents, and needs can make it hard to find meaning and purpose in life. This missed opportunity is knocking on your door. Do not ignore it. Essentially, not embracing your Vibrancy Signature gifts and talents is like having a vibrant, colorful inner garden that you keep hidden and unwatered. Over time, it wilts, leading to a diminished sense of self, emotional struggles, and a life that feels less authentic and fulfilling than it could be.

The journey to confronting these shadow traits involves self-awareness, self-acceptance, and the courageous act of slowly but surely allowing your true, vibrant self to emerge. You deserve to be affirmed and celebrated for stepping into your potent Colorful Vibrancy Powers.

Ready to enlighten yourself? Keep going!

PART TWO

Honoring Your Unique, Colorful Nature

The Five Primary Powers of Your Vibrancy Signature

CHAPTER 5

Your Environment Power

*The First Aspect of Your
Vibrancy Signature*

What if your birth had been honored, and you were seen, appreciated, and welcomed into this world? You'd be a special gift, contributing your soul's light to your family and community. In many cultures, this is what the naming ceremony is all about: a recognition of who you are and an appreciation of what you bring to this world. These conditions ideally shape the first aspect of your personality. You enter the world—your home, family, community, and ultimately your job and social life—in a way that says you are welcomed and honored, and that you belong here.

> As you took your first breath, your first Vibrancy Signature Power enveloped you completely, radiating its unique Colorful Vibrancy Power light. It is a basic part of your personality wiring.

As you took your first breath, your first Vibrancy Signature Power enveloped you completely, radiating its unique Colorful Vibrancy Power light. It is a basic part of your personality wiring.

When you feel accepted and valued by those in your environment, it is easy to grow up offering yourself and generously contributing your talents in a relaxed and magnanimous way. This experience creates a feedback loop of abundance, making you feel connected and enriched by resonating with others around you.

Now imagine sharing your gifts but no one around you notices. This is a tragic situation that, unfortunately, many people encounter, yet it doesn't have to be your story. It's possible to reimagine any early-life scenario as one that's golden, filled with opportunity, and characterized by unconditional love. Seeing yourself through the eyes of your Vibrancy Signature is an ideal way to start.

Introduction to Your Environment Power

The Environment Power is the first of five primary aspects of your Vibrancy Signature, influencing your personality's needs from its environment—both the places you frequent and the people you associate with. With your first breath as a newborn, this coiled pattern of energy flowed through your cells, igniting your nervous system with the "program" it needed to most efficiently coordinate and control all of your bodily functions as its central communication network connecting the rest of your body.

Your Environment Power has a say in all of your life situations. Where do you want to live? What type of work environment is healthy for you? Where do you like to vacation or take time off and have some fun? What kind of people, dispositions, and activities do you want around you? In each case, your nervous system is either unwinding, relaxing, and acting as a free-flowing conduit of energy or it's getting more exhausted, irritated, and less able to do its job as the CEO of your body's processes. Finding your wellness balance point is the ultimate key, and your Environment Power is the one that knows what that feels like.

Whenever you find yourself in a place that nourishes, supports, and validates the healthy attributes of your Environment Power, you will feel relaxed and at peace. Conversely, if your nervous system is out of balance and stressed, it is typically because the people, conversations, and activities around you are rubbing your Environment Power the wrong way. If you feel anxious, nervous, dizzy, or ungrounded, something is either happening or not happening in your surroundings that has disrupted this aspect of your energetic wiring.

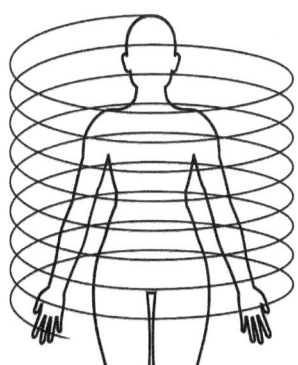

Your Environment Power current determines your resilience and responsiveness to your environment.

Image adapted from Dr. Randolph Stone's "East-West or Air Energy Currents".

As I mentioned earlier, holographic energy patterns are constantly moving throughout your body, much like winding vines in nature. One of these patterns corresponds to your Environment Power and looks like an East-West current, shaped similarly to a coiled spring. Imagine how bumpy the road of life would be without shock absorbers on your vehicle.

This energy pattern in your Vibrancy Signature that you were born with determines the nature of your unique, springy resilience and your responsiveness to your environment. If your life has been a bumpy ride that has left you feeling like your nerves are either overworked and frayed, or underfed and deadened, then you'll want to check in with your Colorful Environment Power. It can provide you with answers on what you need to do to get settled back into your body comfortably. By paying closer attention to this Power to make sure this part of you feels honored, seen, and valued, you'll give your internal shock absorber a new lease on life.

Now let's look at how your Environment Power impacts your psychological health and, subsequently, your physical health.

How Your Environment Power Impacts Your Psychological Health

Imagine trying to decide what to do from the calm center of a storm versus from the storm's edge, where violent winds blow and debris flies. In the first case, you could assess the situation and easily plot your course of action. You'd feel relaxed and comfortably in balance. In the second case, you'd be panicking, nervous, stressed, and unable to make any decision at all, much less a good one. This is what happens when your Environment Power—which resonates with your nervous system health—is out of balance due to duress and stress.

Since you are intrinsically and psychologically connected to this core aspect of your personality, it is impossible to orient yourself and regain your bearings if this part of you is taxed by trying to navigate environments that you can't relax into. And if you try to tolerate this kind of situation for a long time, you could easily develop unique, nervous, and scattered triggers, your body's only way of trying to release the unwanted static in your system. Whenever you experience nervous tension or physical discomfort in your environment, you are very likely not in your ideal surroundings.

Your Environment Vibrancy Power will forever shape your personality and influence the type of environments you're drawn to throughout your life. Ideally, you should live, work, and play in ones that soothe and recharge your nerves, taking their cue from your Colorful Environment Power. If you don't, you will be challenged by constant enervation and scatteredness. When you understand what you need to feel resilient, relaxed, focused, and centered, you will thrive and be able to navigate your life with greater ease and balance.

My Primary Environment Power: Connecting (Indigo Topaz)

I entered this world embodying the Vibrancy Power of Connecting. The light energy associated with this Power is Indigo Topaz. This energy gifted me with the superpower of understanding how different people can learn to appreciate one another, get along, and coexist warmly. You might think of the United Nations or the Olympic rings as symbols of this peaceful coexistence. Unfortunately for me, the community I grew up in was not particularly open to embracing cultural, religious, or social class differences. As a result, I always felt a little disconnected (literally) from my ideal natural environment. When I moved away to college, I finally felt more at peace and relaxed because I was living and engaging in a social melting pot of human differences.

Anyone with this Vibrancy Power is naturally diplomatic and wired with a more spiritual humanitarian nature. You can see why I have loved creating a system that helps us all value one another for our differences. And if you are around me for any length of time, you will see how lit up I am and how at home I feel, when I am able to build bridges of connection with people who have different lifestyles, experiences, and perspectives. A sense of communion and neighborliness is medicine for my nervous system.

If you don't grow up in an environment that supports your true nature, it feels as though something is missing from your life and that you can never quite get comfortable in your own skin. Today, I realize that I thrive most in warm, diplomatic, harmonious environments. Anytime there is bigotry, isolation, or lack of warmth, I am not particularly at ease and know that I need to make the changes necessary to take care of and nurture my Power of Connecting.

How Your Environment Power Impacts Your Physical Health

- Establishes the flow of your nervous system as the first key to your wellbeing

- Fosters a restful night's sleep
- Grounds the electrical circuits flowing through your feet
- Communicates with your organs and glands
- Stimulates neurological communication throughout your body
- Integrates your soul currents from birth to death

Your Environment Power is the key to a good night's sleep and to feeling more at ease by being in the right place. It's critical to pay attention to this aspect of yourself regularly, as it influences the health of your entire nervous system and, in turn, your overall wellbeing.

Any kind of irritation to your nervous system will lead to discomfort (such as agitation, anxiety, or nervousness); a tendency to want to impulsively escape the situation you're in; imbalance in your bodily functions; and, if the cause is not addressed, disease. A more serious situation can occur when you are in the wrong environment for prolonged periods of time. By "wrong" I mean one that doesn't support your needs, welcome your natural style of participation, or allow you to thrive and grow. If you were a plant, you would shrivel and die. For your entire body to function well, you need to find your sense of "this is my place" where your Environment Power can thrive.

Over the years, approximately 30% of my clients have experienced severe stress in their Environment Power, which can ultimately lead to social disconnection and apathy. Some common ways this might manifest physiologically include feelings of dizziness or vertigo. In either case, there is a distortion in the energy pattern of your Environment Power. If you're dizzy, light-headed, faint, woozy, unsteady, or off-balance, it's tough to speak clearly and orient your next step. This can happen when you feel that your insights or what you have to say are not always welcome. An extreme example would be a person in a coma. They clearly felt so unsafe in their environment that their nervous system fractured to the point of fully disassociating from their body. This example is most often related to a severe accident, but not always; whatever the situation, it numbed their Environment Power to some degree. A toxic, dangerous, or upsetting environment is disastrous for one's nervous system health.

During heightened times of nervous system stress, the Environment Power "slinky" energy will move up and out of the body. This phenomenon was the very first problem I sought to solve for my clients and myself. The dissociation, or what I call "dis-integration" of the Environment Power slinky energy, begins at the toes and moves upward toward the crown of the head, sometimes exiting completely as with a coma. The environments you inhabit must ideally allow you to be fully mentally present for smooth energy flow from the crown of your head all the way down to your toes. When you feel calm in your body, initially, your Environment Power energy flows freely through your torso. When you're fully embracing your life and managing your circumstances easily, your nerve energy will flow through your arms. And if you can follow through strongly and never feel as if you're walking on eggshells, your slinky current of energy will flow down your legs and through your toes. As you can imagine, individuals in stressful, abusive, toxic, or dangerous environments become numb and unconscious in these areas throughout their bodies (torso, arms, legs, toes, etc.), at least to some extent.

Just so you have hope for your future: Each of my Vibrancy Signature Powers has, at one time, been partially numbed. Based on my Environment Vibrancy Power, my need to connect with humanity was so strong that when I didn't feel it, I had to go numb to survive. My choice to numb myself began by following my family's patterns of substance abuse. I started with my first cigarette at age 7, my first beer at 8, marijuana at 10, and psychedelics at 14. Over the next six years, I struggled with almost daily narcotic addiction until finally achieving sobriety by age 20. Only when I began placing myself in ideal environments that suited my true nature did I start the process of waking up to heal my nervous system and, ultimately, my Environment Power.

I have immense empathy for anyone who needs to escape their life circumstances and finds their own preferred method of desensitizing themselves to survive, just like I did during these younger years.

The Environment Power in Action: Healing a Broken Arm

I've helped many clients with bone realignments when their energetic pattern became twisted, like a little kid playing too vigorously with their Slinky toy. Aligning the bones orthopedically is not sufficient; if this energy pattern isn't reestablished, the bones won't heal and knit properly.

I worked with a young boy who had a broken radius bone in his forearm; he was still in a great deal of pain even after his cast was removed. Being adept at tracking the movement of energy through the human body, I found that his Environment Power flowed at a

45-degree angle from the break area instead of directly down the arm from the elbow to the wrist. I held the displacement with my right hand and his wrist with my left, quickly identifying the Vibrancy Power stress patterns that he had at the time of the accident and reestablishing proper energy flow all the way to the hand. His pain was immediately better, and there were no further complications from his injury.

By correcting the coiled energy pattern of his Environment Power, I helped ensure the boy's nervous system was fully engaged, present, and flowing properly all the way down to his fingers. This correction provided support for his emotional distress from the pain and aligned his bones properly.

Wrapping It All Up: The Environment Power

Your Environment Power sets the tone when it comes to where you want to live, work, and play and who you share those experiences with. In each case, your nervous system is either unwinding and relaxing or becoming more exhausted and irritated. The secret is to feel at ease in all your environments and create a path of life balance for yourself. Whenever you feel edgy and out of sorts in a situation, it's time to seek a more compatible environment that aligns better with your true nature. What feels right inside you and nourishes your inner self? The more relaxed your nervous system is, the easier it becomes to find your true life path of lightness, balance, and spiritual uplift. This occurs to some extent whenever you're in your ideal environment, because your body is constantly recalibrating from stress and re-centering your nervous system to maintain your overall energetic equilibrium.

It is more important than ever in our fast-paced world to pay attention to any difficulty you have in adequately unwinding and relaxing. These are cues that you need to explore how your nervous system gets recharged and fed by your daily environment. Whether at home, at work, sleeping, or out in the world, you are always surrounded by an environment that needs to nourish your needs. Once you know your Vibrancy Signature Environment Power, you can consciously make choices that are in alignment with that energy, keeping you in harmony and balance.

CHAPTER 6

Your Expression Power
*The Second Aspect of Your
Vibrancy Signature*

Have you ever held a job that made you dread going to work? Plagued by the "Sunday Scaries," you faced each Monday with a familiar pit in your stomach, wishing you could just blink and find it was Friday again.

While work is the primary example of how your Expression Power impacts your life, it also influences other areas where you express your natural talents, such as hobbies and volunteer interests. When you're in balance with this part of you, you engage in your work life with enthusiasm and excitement. However, when your Expression Power is imbalanced—for example, if your parents pushed you to join a sports team in grade school—it would have drained you if, instead, you were happiest engaging in some creative pursuit.

Discovering your right livelihood in life feeds energy, vitality, and purpose to your Expression Power.

If I observe you operating from a part of your personality that doesn't align with your Expression Power gifts, I anticipate that stress and dissatisfaction will be present in your life. Your work should inspire and excite you; it should be something you would pursue even without financial compensation. When you hear someone say, "I actually get paid to do what I love," it's a strong indicator that they are living and working in harmony with their Expression Power talents.

> Discovering your right livelihood in life feeds energy, vitality, and purpose to your Expression Power.

Introduction to the Expression Power

The Expression Power is the second aspect of the Primary Vibrancy Signature. It comes "online" when you turn three months old and begin moving and wiggling in your unique, colorful way. This energy pattern spirals like tree rings and emanates from your belly button.

If you engage your Expression Power gifts in your daily life, you will continue to grow and thrive like a healthy old-growth tree. It impacts the health of your glands, so by nurturing this aspect of your Vibrancy Signature, these specialized systems will be content, enabling your body to continuously regenerate throughout your life.

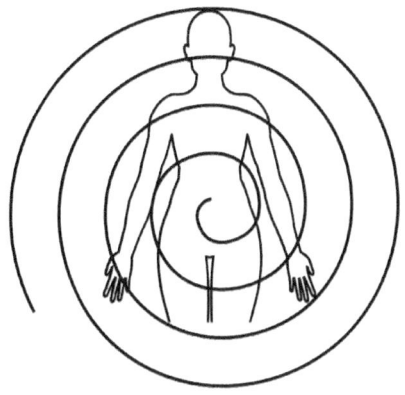

Your Expression Power current spirals like tree rings and emanates from your belly button, helping you thrive like an old-growth tree.

Image adapted from Dr. Randolph Stone's "Spiral or Fire Energy Currents".

It's essential to identify activities, work, and hobbies that resonate with your Vibrancy Signature. When your job doesn't correspond with your Expression Power, you may feel fatigued, unmotivated, and generally dissatisfied with your life.

This aspect of your personality influences your overall energy level. Ideally, you feel enthusiastic and eager to engage in your chosen work or hobby. Hopefully, it's your favorite activity, one that keeps you youthful, nourished, and fully entertained throughout the day. Often it's not, but luckily there are signs that you're out of balance. For example, experiencing boredom, watching the clock, or feeling that your day is a drag is a clear indication that you're not aligned with your Expression Power. Earning a living should originate from what you love to do each day, not from simply fulfilling a specific role. The world needs and values your Expression Power gifts. When you align with and express those gifts, you will feel energized, and others will appreciate your contributions of energy and skills.

Remember that you can retire from a job, but you can never retire from your Expression Power. It's essential to find activities and outlets where you can share this part of your personality. I have seen countless individuals retire without a plan for expressing themselves in the next chapters of their lives, leading to physical and mental decline. You need an outlet for your natural talents, which will continue to rejuvenate you as you contribute to the world in your unique way.

How Your Expression Power Impacts Your Psychological Health

- Gives you the passion to share your skills and talents with the world
- Determines what energizes and engages you
- Sets the stage for spontaneous appreciation from others for your contribution
- Increases your energy level and alertness
- Creates clarity in how you manage your energy expenditures
- Fosters awareness and personal vitality with age

You are ideally wired to find inner harmony and strength with this aspect of your personality. When you go to work and do tasks that don't align with your Expression Power, chances are you'll feel bored, frustrated, and unsatisfied with your job. The good news is that you can consciously start directing your career and activities with clarity and guidance for your future once you fully understand and embrace your Expression Power gifts.

When you develop stable and secure career relationships, they can last a lifetime. Ideally, they will be built on a solid foundation of emotional trust and understanding.

When your internal makeup and external expression in the world are congruent, a secure bond is established. With coworkers, clients, customers, or the public, you will be walking your talk.

This is true because when you fully express your Expression Power gifts, you're in alignment with your energetic blueprint, which defines the daily actions you should take in the world. You are here to pursue your passions and not let anything hinder the contributions that only you can make to the world.

Let's say you receive a promotion at your job, such as transitioning from creative design to managing the creative team. These roles require very different skill sets. If your Vibrancy Expression Power is fed by the creative process, you may find that shifting into a management role is not as enjoyable and maybe even more stressful. Likewise, if you're energetically wired for leadership, you'll be energized by this step up in your career. It's important for your contentment and health to zero in on the gifts that are yours to bring into your workplace or hobbies, and to make career choices that highlight them. Always seek a win-win scenario for yourself. Making more money holds little real value if it comes at the cost of excessive stress or a lack of creative fulfillment. Your priorities belong to you. The happiest people in the world love their work and typically do not experience issues with financial insecurity. As you express your unique gifts, the world will respond, contribute, and show gratitude for your talents. Just discover what you love to do, and you will naturally pursue it with enthusiasm and joy.

My Primary Expression Power: Aliveness (Lapis Blue)

This Power is all about waking people up with dynamic energy. Whether from stage, on the phone, in writing or in the office, this energy wants to lift and enliven others to tap into and shine more of their natural radiant light.

You might remember that I wanted to be a singing doctor when I grew up. And guess what? Every day during my healing sessions with clients, I sing specific affirmations that relate to healing their stress patterns. Then they sing them right back to me as we establish a new, vibrant healing direction for their lives. Luckily, I have found my ideal life calling. The name of my business, The Vibrancy Path, was inspired by my desire to work somewhere that made me feel alive and vibrant each day.

My favorite activity is identifying places where my clients have shut down their vitality and then teaching and directing them to repattern their life activities toward a more vital and life-affirming direction. The only time I felt out of sync with my Power of Aliveness was when I was solely doing energetic body work on my clients. While I really enjoyed working with them (after all, my Environment Power thrives on connection), I always felt exhausted by the end of the day. After paying closer attention to the wisdom of my Vibrancy Signature, I realized that it might be because I was not using my Expression Power. Instead, I was serving my clients only from my Intimacy Power gifts, which is the next aspect you will learn about. This resulted in draining myself personally because I was not recharging with my Expression Power of Aliveness, which is fed by teaching, coaching, and guiding people through their healing journeys, as I do now.

How Your Expression Power Impacts Your Physical Health

- Provides physical regeneration and youthfulness in your glandular system
- Creates a steady flow of energy throughout your day
- Encourages an effortless pattern of self-healing
- Improves your natural vitality as you age
- Enables your body to continually feel strong and youthful
- Supports all your body parts to function and thrive through all life phases

Not only will you feel mentally energized and nourished by engaging in work that nurtures this aspect of your Vibrancy Signature, you'll also feel great physically. In fact, the right livelihood or hobbies are crucial for sustaining energy throughout your life. When you see someone's body collapsing, shutting down, or deteriorating, it often relates to their Expression Power lacking sufficient outgoing engagement.

Think of yourself as a kid heading out to the playground. Are you dragging yourself along, feeling lifeless or generally unmotivated because there's nothing going on out there that excites you? Or do you know exactly what you're up to, so you have endless energy to express yourself and enjoy what you are doing? This is possible for you when you calibrate and align your Expression Power.

So how can you restore your natural zest and energy if you're not feeling particularly lively? You begin by understanding the gifts and needs of your Expression Power. What role does it play in your life?

Mine is to help others connect with a dynamic sense of being alive. What does this Power need from me? Since I embody the Power of Aliveness, I need to avoid holding back my own expression of vitality, and I must remember that people primarily come to me to experience the energy flowing through my cells. When they do, they will feel more energized to do the same for themselves.

Whatever your Vibrancy Power, know that it is the primary energy that the world needs you to share and wake up in them. Your Expression Power is medicine for those you are serving through your work and who might be lacking the energy you embody. You're also a partner for those who radiate that same Power and, likewise, are here to uplift the world with this special energy. Your job is to find the right career or volunteer scenario where this part of you is needed and can show up in all its fullness. At the end of the day (not too short a day and not too long), you will return to your personal life satisfied and ready to wake up to another day of fulfillment.

It is your glands that regenerate your body and keep you vibrant. This is why you often see people who love their work never retiring; they just keep going. I once watched a documentary about famous octogenarian rock stars that illustrates this point well. They seemed to have as much fun as their 30-year-old selves and moved with a similar zest and passion for life.

This is possible for you when your livelihood fully aligns with what you want to share with the world. Is it your brilliant ideas, creative ingenuity, or youthful playfulness? Maybe it's your adventurous spirit, intellectual acumen, or simply your caring and nurturing nature. Whatever is wired into this aspect of your Vibrancy Signature is meant to be your life calling. Your Expression Power must align with your daily life, serving as a source of fun and enjoyment as you enter the world's playground with your unique talents.

The Expression Power in Action: Dying of Laughter

One of my clients Joseph had the Vibrancy Power of Laughter (Lemon) as his Expression Power. He was in the process of taking over the family funeral business. Lemon energy is all about bringing levity to any situation, providing comic relief to even the most difficult situations. It's an energy that helps soften the rough edges of life, and it is often considered an antidote for grief and any feelings of despair. So in his mission at the family business, if Joseph could specialize in bringing joy, celebration of life, and lighthearted stories to their funeral services, he would be more energetic and authentically in alignment with his career path.

Unfortunately, his family was not supportive of his often-witty career talents and the direction he wished to take the business. They did not think his suggestions were very funny, so he finally let the family business go and began pursuing a career at a performance art academy. This is another example of how your future vitality and youthfulness are directly linked to enjoying what you do every day in your livelihood. Make sure that, just like Joseph, you choose to honor your gifts that feed your Expression Power nature. Only then can you feel a sense of energy and rightness with what you do on a day-to-day basis.

Wrapping It All Up: The Expression Power

Here's a vital truth, courtesy of your Expression Power: As you get older, there's no reason for you to decay or degenerate…or to stop doing what you love, whether for work, as a hobby, or as a favorite activity. Yes, chronological aging occurs, but most of my clients feel younger and more vibrant once they start living in alignment with their Vibrancy Expression Power, regardless of age. When you align your life with this Power, you naturally feel inclined to share your colorful gifts as often as possible through a well-chosen vocation or avocation. You have the potential to radiate your powerful talents to the world, enjoy yourself, make a difference, and prosper through all your contributions.

Ideally, your Expression Power will inspire enthusiasm in you, allowing you to spread that excitement to anyone who is drawn to your work, whether it's a job or a passion project. It's time for you to consistently love what you do and feel younger with each passing day that you engage in it. When it comes to the Expression Power aspect of your personality, you thrive when you're engaging in activities that nourish and excite you—those that you can't wait to get back to soon.

CHAPTER 7

Your Intimacy Power

The Third Aspect of Your Vibrancy Signature

How do you experience love? Do you give and receive it freely, to others and to yourself? I use the word *love* as shorthand for all the aspects of human connection: support, understanding, care, and closeness.

Your Intimacy Power reflects a vital aspect of your personality that supports you in a literal sense, providing the foundation you need to stand tall and embrace your life and the people in it. You are energetically wired to withstand life's pressures and to seek support when necessary. When you feel the need to laugh, cry, talk to a friend, or seek a hug and companionship, your Intimacy Power within you reaches out for love and support, and it influences how you experience care, love, and feeling understood by others in a deeply personal way. It also affects how you give your love, care, and understanding to others close to you.

Conversely, when you keep people at a distance, it's often because this part of you hesitates to form a close personal connection. This may feel too challenging or unsafe, or you might find yourself too vulnerable to share your personal history or reveal your wounds or vulnerabilities.

Your Intimacy Power represents how you most easily express closeness, tenderness, support, and mutual understanding with others.

> Your Intimacy Power represents how you most easily express closeness, tenderness, support, and mutual understanding with others.

Any person whom you don't feel a loving connection to is someone you'll keep at arm's length. Think of a business handshake with a new client or customer versus a bear hug with a family member or old friend. It also determines which forms of the expressions of love, care, and support touch you the most deeply. What if engaging in deep conversations is what fills your heart with love for your partner, but you only receive a periodic bouquet of flowers with few words shared in your day-to-day? You won't feel the love nearly as strongly as you would if you regularly enjoyed long conversations together.

Last but not least, your Intimacy Power also determines how you experience this same level of intimacy with yourself. Even though it is the most important of all, it is often overlooked. At times, you might find it easier to share your love with someone else before you're ready to extend it to yourself, but your Intimacy Power wants you to feel loved from all directions and will keep knocking on your door until you do.

Introduction to the Intimacy Power

The third aspect of your Vibrancy Signature is your Intimacy Power. Each time you seek a close bond with someone, it is your Intimacy Power that reaches out. Conversely, when you feel a lack of love or support, you're experiencing an imbalance in your Intimacy Power. And don't let the term *intimacy* fool you—it encompasses not just partners or children but also friends, coworkers, and anyone with whom you share a personal and meaningful connection.

Your Intimacy Power represents the facet of your personality that connects you with others and reflects how you tend to your needs for close connection. In many ways, this is the part of your personality that determines how you feel seen, supported, and truly understood.

The Intimacy Power manifests by the time you are six months old, when you are stretching out to the people in your world to be held, loved, and supported. You have 10 distinct longitudinal energy circuits pulsing through your body and flowing through your fingers and toes. Your ability to withstand gravitational pressure is due to this energy pattern keeping you upright.

The Vibrancy Signature

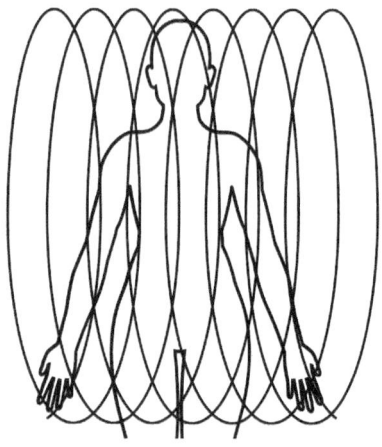

Your Intimacy Power current connects you with others and reflects how you tend to your needs for close connection.

Image adapted from Dr. Randolph Stone's "Longitudinal or Water Currents".

Whenever you feel scared, abused, hurt, misunderstood, betrayed, or abandoned, a personal deflation occurs, collapsing this part of your energetic wiring. This happens because, as a human being, you always need certain relationships to act as mirrors in your life, helping to lift you up, be sensitive to your vulnerabilities, and encourage your growth and maturity. Sometimes, it can be easy to live in isolation, or maybe with a trusty pet who provides you with unconditional love, as you may not feel the need to share your personal wounds and insecurities. However, the moment you reach out from this aspect of your personality, personal growth and evolution begin in your life. This is why relationships and close connections with other people can be the most challenging—they confront the core issues of your humanity.

Are you loved, supported, seen, and valued?

Do you have people in your life who perceive you as special, precious, and beautiful?

We often want to distract ourselves from answering these questions, but understanding the part that your Intimacy Power plays in your personal journey opens the door to awakening and discovering deep inner support for your happiness and spiritual growth. Whenever you feel yourself collapsing inward or struggling to handle life's pressures, look to your Intimacy Power for guidance on how to experience more support, understanding, and love in your life.

How Your Intimacy Power Impacts Your Psychological Health

- Determines how you feel supported, loved, and understood
- Provides for self-esteem and empowerment within your life experiences
- Establishes emotional security and ease for physical intimacy
- Enables you to be vulnerable, honest, and openhearted
- Inspires your willingness to grow and mature in relationship dynamics
- Helps you to repattern personal stress with a courageous mindset

As you might imagine, when this intimacy aspect is out of balance, you'll experience a range of challenging feelings: unworthiness, being "less than," and being alone in the world. You'll fear getting close to another person because they may confirm what you think about yourself.

Think about the psychological toll this can take, as you could spend your whole life hiding, being alone, and refusing personal contact. This would keep you stuck, unable to evolve and live your potential. And it doesn't even have to be so pronounced—you could be very personable with work colleagues, for instance, but they may know nothing about your personal talents, gifts, or interests.

> Once you discover your Intimacy Power, you'll have a better understanding of how to create psychological safety in interpersonal relationships.

Once you discover your Intimacy Power, you'll have a better understanding of how to create psychological safety in interpersonal relationships.

It's the key aspect of your Vibrancy Signature that can help you feel supported, internally full, and able to courageously face life experiences with ease, support, and harmony.

My Primary Intimacy Power: Healing (Crystal)

I spent 14 years sharing my Intimacy Power talents with clients, unknowingly neglecting to reserve that energy for my personal life with friends and my first two wives. People with this Power in their Vibrancy Signature have the natural ability to redirect or free up blocked energy. During this time, I was seeing clients for hands-on healing therapy. At the end of the day, when I should have been hugging, massaging, and physically connecting with my wife, I had already channeled that energy to my clients. I had nothing left for closeness because it had been spent on my clients' needs.

Once I learned the lesson of how to use my Intimacy Power gifts wisely, I stopped providing hands-on bodywork for clients, reserving that healing physical contact for my dogs, cats, and, most importantly, my beautiful wife Chaya.

You can see how knowing your Vibrancy Signature Powers can save you a lot of heartache and pain, while at the same time giving you the possibility of a great life!

Whenever you face a personal crisis, drama, or internal angst, check in with your Intimacy Power to understand what's happening. Naturally, you may bury deep-seated wounds, issues, and life experiences in your Intimacy Power "closets." Therefore, as you commit to confronting these issues, it may be beneficial to seek out safe friends, partners, or therapists to assist in your personal-growth journey.

Since I have the Intimacy Power of Healing (Crystal), I enjoy bodywork, and I've consistently been able to unwind trauma, tension, and deep wounds with the assistance of skilled body/mind practitioners. It's important to consider the self-healing methods that your Intimacy Power indicates as safest and most revitalizing. You deserve to feel protected and encouraged in cultivating closeness on your personal-growth journey.

How Your Intimacy Power Impacts Your Physical Health

- Provides daily support and healthy function for your organ systems
- Ensures your internal circulation vitality
- Supports your good posture and flexibility
- Enables you to recharge from pain or stiffness
- Promotes inner peace and your physical harmony
- Helps you maintain youthful energy

Throughout the energetic rhythm of your day, your Intimacy Power needs replenishing, support, and recharging for you to face another day feeling nourished inside, and so that you're drawing from a full well. You have an internal responsibility to give yourself the attention, time, and love you need, and then to be present for opportunities to enhance the day of those close to you with your caring nature. When you take the time to engage in your favorite activity, you're giving yourself a dose of self-love and nurturing. Look for what provides that for you daily. For some people, it's their personal prayer, mindfulness, or meditation practice. You might recharge by walking in nature, running and exercising, cooking your favorite meal, getting a massage, playing your favorite music, singing or jamming with friends, drawing or painting, building something from your imagination, or simply having some quiet contemplative time. In this fast-paced world, it's easy to get caught up in life's demands and forget to take care of yourself along the way. Your Intimacy Power is here to remind you how to best attend to your personal needs and support your wellbeing every day.

As you practice self-care, your Intimacy Power influences the health of each of your organs and keeps them functioning optimally. Just as you seek support and closeness, your organs also require your attention. When you neglect your relationships, they tend to fall apart. The same is true for your organ health; any self-neglect leads to internal collapsing and shutting down.

Each organ plays a specific role in providing internal support to keep you going.

- Breathing life into each day (lungs)
- Allowing in openness, vulnerability, and kindness (heart)
- Processing life experiences; easily releasing toxic people or situations (liver)
- Welcoming nourishing feedback; releasing emotional stress (lymphatic system)

Whenever you feel alone, unsupported, or overwhelmed by life's pressures, you're heading down a dangerous path. Your organs remain healthy when you muster the inner courage to face life's challenges with daily constructive actions. A lack of healthy action is one of the greatest obstacles to your health.

This is the main reason organ failure is so rampant in the world. You deserve to be close and to be loved. If you don't have a healthy relationship with your Vibrancy Signature Intimacy Power, it's difficult to feel worthy of love and attention, and to practice self-care. When you pay attention to your personal needs, your organs are influenced by the degree of your inner happiness. Each time you struggle, feel unsupported, or whine about your life, you need some Intimacy Power attention. When you support these vulnerable areas, you also enhance the health and strength of your organs.

One final note about your physical health and your Intimacy Power energy patterns: They are connected to posture. If you're hunched over or getting shorter, this indicates an intimate life that has not had enough support and is collapsing due to the heaviness of life experiences. The antidote is to surround yourself with beautiful, nourishing food, friends, and family support. You deserve to find intimacy and emotional closeness in your life and to give yourself what you need to fill up with support, care, and love.

The Intimacy Power in Action: Smooth Sailing for Couples

With couples, when you discover your true Intimacy Power needs and talents, you can share them with your partner and find ways to be there for each other.

One of my couple clients had opposing yet vibrant strengths, and by understanding each other's needs, they found a compatible direction to pursue together. The wife had the Power of Prevention (Sea Blue) as her primary Intimacy Power, which led her to seek the safest, healthiest, and most caring path in life. Her husband had the Power of Courage (Mango) as his primary Environment Power, making him eager for the next fun adventure and life challenge. He proposed taking his young kids and wife on a sailing adventure for a year. She immediately responded, "No way—it's too dangerous." However, they eventually devised a plan and reached a compromise to mutually support each other's "colorful" needs. They located the safest boat possible, avoided severe weather challenges whenever they could, and of course, steered clear of areas known to have pirates and other unsafe characters. Ultimately, they enjoyed a wonderful and safe adventure, creating memories that would last a lifetime.

By appreciating the differences in your Vibrancy Signature, you and your partner can be the rare exception who consistently find compromise, understanding, forgiveness, and a willingness to keep growing while supporting the path each of you wishes to pursue together. This journey can be one of the most amazing aspects of your Intimacy Power experience, allowing you to compatibly share your ups and downs and foster a deep, loving connection.

Wrapping It All Up: The Intimacy Power

You deserve all the support you need to live life according to your personal goals, dreams, and desires. Ideally, you can build relationships with people who love and appreciate your unique self and provide encouragement for you to live authentically. These kinds of close and meaningful relationships nourish and uplift both partners. This is only achievable when you understand your personal Intimacy Power needs and those of your friends, family, and partners.

Because you're wired in a unique way, it's easier to recognize that each of your relationships has its own preferences and strategies for feeling secure and loved. In your intimate relationships, you'll need to feel confident about your sexuality, finances, and homemaking routines, for example. You'll bring your preferences, but you must also be willing to compromise with your partner to ensure that both of you can have your needs met as effectively as possible. When you truly understand your partner's needs (which is much easier when you know their Vibrancy Signature), you'll naturally want to ensure their happiness and fulfillment. I've worked with couples married for 50 years who tell their spouse, "Now I get who you really are."

And once you know your Intimacy Power, you'll finally know how to keep yourself grounded. Everything you do in relationships with others (and even yourself!) becomes much easier and less adversarial. This approach allows for conversations instead of arguments. It provides an opportunity to consciously create harmony and connection without unreasonable expectations. When you fully understand yourself and those you wish to share your life with, you are much more likely to "play" together with joy and warmth, and in sweet harmony.

CHAPTER 8

Your Life Force Power

*The Fourth Aspect of Your
Vibrancy Signature*

Before we explore your Life Force Power, let's make a quick mental visit to a baseball field. Imagine your favorite ballpark, your hometown team, and a brilliant sunny day. Your team is on the field, prepared for anything that comes their way.

Suddenly, you notice the pitcher doing something unusual. He chooses not to throw the ball to the batter. The game comes to a halt, leaving all the other players on your team unable to play and perform their designated positions.

In this analogy, consider your Vibrancy Signature Powers as your team and the pitcher as your Life Force Power. It's what animates everyone. But to do so, it must be ready, willing, and able to play ball with the whole team—starting with the other four aspects of your Primary Vibrancy Signature. While you're learning about each aspect individually, it's this fourth aspect that drives a crucial point home.

Your Life Force Power influences your will to live and willingness to get up each day and face your life with joy and purpose.

> Your Life Force Power influences your will to live and willingness to get up each day and face your life with joy and purpose.

Every facet of your existence is influenced by your Life Force Power. When this Power loses its connection to your unique purpose and stops fully "pitching the ball," you lose your inner drive to play the game of your life. Once you thoroughly understand each of these aspects of yourself, you can navigate your life through conscious choices rather than by chance. You can choose a supportive environment, a satisfying career, and a nurturing personal life that all work harmoniously with your Life Force aspect, allowing you to remain fully engaged in your vibrant, brilliant life.

Introduction to the Life Force Power

This fourth aspect of your Primary Vibrancy Signature—your Life Force Power—is essentially your inner "battery." It is what energizes your senses that, in turn, engages you in having a day filled with passion and energy.

Your Life Force Power flows through your body as an incredible helical pattern of energy resembling the DNA helix, which vibrates throughout every joint, energizing your senses and coursing up and down your spinal column. You can tell your battery is running low if you find yourself losing passion in life and feeling sluggish when getting up in the morning. Engaging with others in an uplifting and life-affirming manner is the hallmark of your Life Force Power.

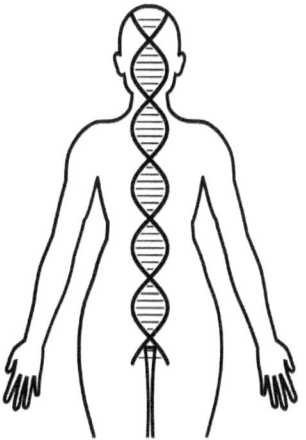

Your Life Force Power current influences your will to live and vibrates throughout every joint, energizing your senses and coursing up and down your spinal column.

Image adapted from Dr. Randolph Stone's "Double Helix Current".

This aspect of your Vibrancy Signature is intertwined with your will to live and infuses your life with imagination and meaning. It was anchored inside you when you turned nine months old, when you were crawling to touch everything within reach.

Your Life Force Power inspires you to look with fascination, hear with wonder, and explore with awe and joy. Because this aspect of your makeup is so crucial for being fully engaged in your life, it can be seen as the captain of your personality team, ensuring that all the other players are on board and working smoothly together in your life. It fuels the inner spark that each of your other Vibrancy Powers needs to function and thrive, and it reenergizes and recharges those first three primary aspects of your Vibrancy Signature. Now let's look at the relationship between your Life Force Power and your Environment Power.

Life Force Power Meets Environment Power

As I mentioned earlier, your Environment Power influences the health of your nervous system, helping your body relax and feel invigorated. When your Life Force Power teams up with your Environment Power, it provides the energy needed to regenerate your body and nerves. It is what keeps you mentally sharp and attuned to the world around you.

When Life Force Power and Environment Power are balanced: You will greet each day with enthusiasm, engaging with whatever your Life Force Power passionately desires to embrace fully. You will feel alive and alert, and experience vitality flowing through all your senses.

When Life Force Power and Environment Power are out of balance, blocked, or diminished: Your neurological firing will gradually suppress, and you will begin to lose the inclination to communicate with the world around you. Your eyes will become dimmer, your hearing fuzzy, and your thinking sluggish, all because you have lost some of the passion for why you are here on this planet.

Whenever I assist someone in troubleshooting their psychological or physical life challenges, it's always heavily influenced by how well they manage their Life Force Power and overall Vibrancy

Signature. Often, personal stresses and disconnects began earlier in life when some aspect of their personality was not recognized or lovingly validated. After all, it's natural for others around you to perceive you through their own filters, values, and interests.

Each of us has a unique baseline personality. Even if others miss that and don't support it, you can achieve life balance just by listening to what you authentically want and need. Each part of you possesses its own desires, interests, and personal preferences. Your healthiest relationships will be with people who truly see and understand you.

The more you comprehend yourself, the easier it becomes to let others in on the secret of who you are. In an ideal world, you would have no secrets; you would declare from the rooftops, "This is who I am!" This is especially true for the gifts of your Life Force Power, since it is the driving force in your life.

Life Force Power Meets Expression Power

Your Expression Power influences your choice of livelihood and hobbies as well as the way your Life Force Power battery fuels your ability to work with vigor and vitality.

When Life Force Power and Expression Power are balanced: You are energized and fully engaged, which your Expression Power loves. This allows you to work at full throttle, keeping your body and mind continually regenerated while preventing premature aging and various degenerative health conditions. These two aspects of your personality are the dynamic duo that keeps you young, vital, and passionate about what you do every day to contribute to the world.

When Life Force Power and Expression Power are out of balance, blocked, or diminished: You will experience shutdown, aging, and premature degeneration. On both a glandular and psychic level, when you feel bored or unmotivated or lose passion for life, it means your Life Force Power and Expression Power are out of balance, not working together, and negatively impacting your overall vitality and productivity.

Whenever you have the chance to share your Life Force Power passion, your eyes light up, you pay close attention, and your voice radiates dynamic energy. Everything you do becomes better and more fulfilling when your Life Force Power joins the mix. When people are less engaged, they tend to withdraw from conversations or simply do not enjoy their surroundings. Therefore, it's essential to check in with yourself to ensure you are participating in activities and connecting with individuals who allow your Life Force Power talents to shine. You may not achieve 100% passionate engagement, but you should aim for 90% aliveness, which is especially important for your significant relationships, both personal and professional.

Life Force Power meets Intimacy Power

Are you ready to march forward into a new relationship paradigm? One in which you can be understood quickly and are appreciated and valued for what you bring to the table in life and relationships? When your Life Force Power and Intimacy Power are potent when they work in concert, developing a relationship of true closeness and harmony.

When Life Force Power and Intimacy Power are balanced: You are passionate and motivated to bring life energy, aliveness, and a spark to what you do and who you do it with—feeding and nurturing your personal desires. Your natural love strategy occurs when the energy of these two aspects brings closeness and passion together within you simultaneously.

When Life Force Power and Intimacy Power are out of balance, blocked, or diminished: You have difficulty understanding someone you truly want to connect with—you just can't relate or get on the same wavelength. Closeness without passion is just physical connection. It is missing the spark of your whole self, which your Life Force Power provides (when it's not blocked or out of balance).

How Your Life Force Power Impacts Your Psychological Health

- Ignites your will to live and ability to face your life with ease
- Helps keep you wide open to life experiences
- Provides you with the willingness to take in life responsively and effortlessly
- Drives your enthusiasm for evolving and embracing new opportunities
- Enables you to feel free to move through life smoothly like a dance
- Continually expands your inner awareness

When you find your passion, you'll want to be fully present in your life. Therefore, the most important question to ask yourself is "Do I want to be here? And if so, why?"

Because your Life Force Power influences your will to live, it carries profound psychological implications. If you engage fully in your life, you'll move effortlessly and joyfully through the world. However, that might not be your everyday reality. If you're like most people, your life is good at times and not so good at others, and on any given day you might be indecisive.

Your Life Force Power prepares you to face your day with aliveness and passion.

> Your Life Force Power prepares you to face your day with aliveness and passion.

Do you wake up regularly with enthusiasm and excitement? When you keep your inner battery recharging, you'll find it easier to feel motivated, passionate, and fully engaged in your life. This has nothing to do with your age but everything to do with discovering your Life Force Power passions and living them daily. I feel younger today than I did at 30 because I've learned how to honor my Life Force Power and core self by allowing it to guide the activities of my daily life journey.

One of your most fundamental psychological needs is figuring out how to feel secure within this core aspect of your personality. Let's start with how you feel loved and understood. This becomes much easier when you have a deep understanding of your Life Force Power, as it clarifies your internal passion for life. It helps enhance any relationship, particularly personal ones, when you comprehend what matters to the other, what makes them feel valued, what motivates them, and how they feel deeply understood. The foundation of any relationship is a stable and secure understanding of one another, as well as a shared appreciation of your fundamental needs that make you feel alive and loved. For some partnerships, this can take decades and may still feel rocky and unclear. Knowing this aspect of your Vibrancy Signature can again relieve undue stress, emotional and psychological turmoil, and other negative impacts within yourself and in the context of your primary relationships.

Your Life Force Power rhythm influences your spinal flow, extending from your lower back sacrum to the base of your skull. This is where the Life Force Power engine for your brain resides. Senility and a variety of mental disorders are associated with trying to shut out what doesn't make sense through your life filters. You can always learn from your difficulties, mistakes, and choices and discover how to "reboot" the engine that drives your mind. This is possible when you let your Life Force Power flow effortlessly through you each day.

Whenever you're secure with your Life Force Power personality dynamics, you're also secure in your life and spiritual values. Your personal and professional desires extend beyond physical accomplishments, monetary success, and public notoriety to include spiritual maturation as you evolve into your full humanity. With this kind of spiritual grounding, you feel grateful, peaceful, and present in your relationships. This is achievable when you align with your Life Force Power. By doing so, you'll cultivate cherished relationships based on trust, where you feel completely seen and understood.

My Primary Life Force Power: Growing (Red Gold)

Let me share with you my colorful Red Gold Life Force Power: the Power of Growing. This represents my core passion for life.

To thrive, I need personal growth, business growth, relationship growth, spiritual growth, and environments filled with people who continue to develop, mature, and evolve. Sometimes, we learn to embrace our true nature by first exploring the opposite shadow-path direction. For me, that period mostly spanned ages 10 to 20.

During that period, I didn't know how to transform and grow. Instead, I knew how to lie, steal, cheat, escape, run away, and go into avoidance. I didn't know how to embrace my capacity to evolve into a healthier version of myself. Instead, I found that numbing and looking away from the truth seemed easier and less painful, and it gave me a few moments of relief. Since my early twenties, I've attempted to consciously and continually grow, facing the reality and truth of my life circumstances.

No matter how stuck, anguish-filled, or disheartened I became, I always knew I had a secret superpower to transform my history or current life situation. You have your own Life Force superpower too. Along the way and over the decades, I've found ways to help each of my clients grow, regenerate, and discover their personal-growth truth and core passions.

Mine is a paradigm-shifting Power that moves me to leave my past behind once and for all and embrace my next step of evolution. If I find myself degenerating in any way, I know that the solution is to simply lean into the light of my Life Force Power and begin to transform and grow into a new, healthier reality.

My favorite Red Gold motto is "The truth will set me free." I now dislike being stuck in old patterns so much that my wife Chaya says that sometimes, even within a day, she can see a new version of me emerge.

When you're aligned with your Life Force Power, you'll move your own mountains in your unique way, gifting and even infusing others in your world with this energy.

How Your Life Force Power Impacts Your Physical Health

- Promotes your joint health and ease of movement
- Supports your eyesight and hearing functions
- Keeps you cognitively alert and aware
- Maintains your spinal and neurological health
- Ensures your lifelong physical wellness
- Gives you the motivation and energy to get your body moving each day

The inner battery that is your life force is crucial for your physical health as it relates to your joints and senses. If your Life Force Power is compromised, your joints begin to stiffen, your eyesight and hearing may deteriorate, and you can end up losing the battery of your mind, possibly leading to senility. This illustrates why engaging your Life Force Power is one of the secrets to a healthy and vibrant life.

When you feel less gusto, every day that passes will impact some part of your body. It's possible that your toes may become a little stiffer, or your shoulders a little tighter. Every joint in your body represents a place where you want to dance to the music of your life. When you simply go through the motions and disengage from the Life Force Power aspect of your personality, you tune out and run your life with minimal energy. This occurs when you choose to abandon your core desires, which vibrationally resonate throughout your body.

So start by taking a joint inventory to identify where you're feeling stuck. Consider your hips, which encourage you to "dance through life" and guide you to what you are passionate about. Notice your knees, which empower you to navigate life's challenges gracefully. Ideally, your ankles and toes feel grateful as you take the next steps in your life, embracing change and pursuing a healthier direction. When conflicting scenarios play out in your mind, your body may eventually signal for help through stiffness and pain, potentially requiring joint replacements to keep moving. Any inflamed, arthritic, stiff, numb, or misshapen joint often signifies "war and struggle" in following your Life Force Power priorities.

Next, consider how sharp (or not) your senses are. Part of the joy of living is listening to music, hearing a baby laugh, or enjoying the birds chirping around you. You can take in a glorious sunset, watch the clouds create beautiful shapes above you, or gaze into the eyes of someone you love. You can smell a fragrant rose, savor the aroma of your favorite meal, or simply appreciate the scent of fresh rain. Your Life Force Power orchestrates your senses: hearing, seeing, and smelling, along with taste, touch, and intuition. You can learn to cooperate with your senses and allow them to filter their feedback instead of blocking the input coming your way. When your senses wane, it signals the story building inside you, one of tuning out rather than tuning in. If you've ever said to yourself or others "I can't even hear that" or "I can't see that anymore," your body takes these internal commands seriously and makes them reality.

When your captain, the pitcher on your Vibrancy Signature team, gives up trying to enjoy your life by playing the part you've been given, it becomes easier for the rest of your team to follow suit. Life isn't meant to be easy; it's an adventure where you can discover the "magical mystery tour" that your Vibrancy Powers are designed to take. (Yes, I grew up listening to The Beatles, if you were wondering.) Your Life Force Power enlivens these passions in life and brings all the players on your Vibrancy Signature team the energy each of them needs to shine brightly.

Wrapping It All Up: The Life Force Power

Your body always yearns to move, dance, feel alive, discover life's purpose, and express gratitude for this gift of life. The flow of your Life Force Power energy accomplishes that, keeping your physical and inner senses energized and engaged.

You deserve to envision a brighter future, hear the songs that inspire you, savor the flavors of life, and relish the clarity of your own mental faculties. This is only achievable when you befriend your Life Force Power, grant yourself permission to discover your passion, and allow it to flow through your very being. The essence of your personality inspires others through your vibrant enthusiasm, youthful spirit, and the unique Life Force Power gifts you share with the world.

CHAPTER 9

Your Intention Power

*The Fifth Aspect of Your
Vibrancy Signature*

For the fifth primary aspect of your Vibrancy Signature, let's take a quick mental detour. Think about your all-time favorite television show or movie series (James Bond, for example). Does the theme song play automatically in your mind?

Just as the brilliant music of a television show or film ties everything together, sets the tone, conveys passion for the subject, and communicates core beliefs, sensibilities, preferences, and overall ethos, the Intention Power is the theme music of your life. Everywhere you go and everything you do is influenced by your Intention Power. Wouldn't it be wonderful to trust and honor your intentions throughout your life?

So set an intention now as you explore this final aspect of your Primary Vibrancy Signature. Let's agree that the path to happiness, success, and fulfillment requires you to discover the ideal balance of all five primary aspects of your Vibrancy Signature. When asked which colorful Power is the most important, I often joke, "Which of your five kids do you want to be happy and nourished?" The radiant, colorful circuitry that animates your body is uniquely dynamic.

The energetic dance of all your Vibrancy Signature Powers exists to express your authentic voice and unique contribution to the world.

The healthier these patterns flow in harmony with your creative gifts and talents, and the more their needs are met, the more vibrant your life engagement and inner vitality become. Your task is to uncover your own unique story of happiness and life direction.

> The energetic dance of all your Vibrancy Signature Powers exists to express your authentic voice and unique contribution to the world.

Now, let's tie everything together with your Vibrancy Signature's theme song source: your Intention Power.

Introduction to the Intention Power

Last but certainly not least, in your Primary Vibrancy Signature, your Intention Power is the fifth aspect. This radiant pattern of energy flows through every tissue in your body and transmits every thought and emotion to your trillions of cells. This is why I describe this aspect of your Vibrancy Signature as the theme music of your life.

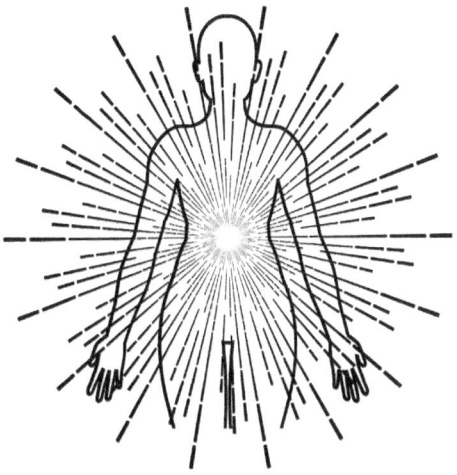

Your Intention Power current transmits every thought and emotion to your trillions of cells, acting as the theme song of your life.

When your body tissues lose coherence and elasticity, or feel painful constriction, it's generally because this vital part of your personality has been suppressed, or you've become distracted from what's important to you. This is quite common and leads to living according to others' expectations and demands while neglecting your own personal autonomy and disregarding your clear life path. Here's what it looks like when your other Powers dance with this aspect.

Intention Power meets Environment Power

Look at your nerve circulation in your body and see how well you're following your Intention and Environment Powers in a harmonious fashion. Your nerve tissues are directing you to follow your life music and relax into the beat of your own drum. If you ignore this internal relationship, you'll experience a deadening and numbing of your neurological health and vitality.

When Intention Power and Environment Power are balanced: Every moment, you are contemplating a direction that you wish to follow next in your life. These two aspects keep you attuned to your life direction along with your personal goals, life ambitions, spiritual discoveries, and the inner awakening of your dreams or true desires. Life is filled with interest and opportunity when your Intention Power flows dynamically through your Environment Power, and you are awakened to why you are here on the planet.

When Intention Power and Environment Power are out of balance, blocked, or diminished: At times, you may feel nothing, numbness, or a lack of personal direction. During this shutting-down process, you find yourself disconnected from your source of inner clarity and your life road map. You're aimlessly going through the motions of your life without paying much attention to what you feel or experience. This is like horror films where zombies take over. You instead deserve to be alert, conscious, in charge, and directing your life from your highest internal calling. This becomes possible when you activate your Intention Power, give it permission to direct your next life decision through your Environment Power, and begin enlivening your daily journey.

From your first birthday to your last trip around the sun, you possess a unique light Power that needs to be shared with others. Each birthday can ideally serve as a reminder of what your Intention Power is here to share and celebrate. It is a beautiful, colorful circuitry animating your body tissues. It's as if the canvas of your life radiates your Intention Power light to the world.

Intention Power meets Expression Power

Once again, your Expression Power is the expressive energy behind finding your life of service to the world. When you combine your Intention Power with your Expression Power you have a dynamic duo that finds the theme of how you wish to impact and bring your talents to others. There is a congruence and natural vitality in your life when these aspects of your Vibrancy Signature work together smoothly.

When Intention Power and Expression Power are balanced: You will be directed to follow your overall life design in your daily work. When your Intention Power joins forces with your Expression Power, you'll naturally amplify the impact of what you can offer to your community. You'll not only feel energized with what you are doing, but also have a clear sense of "rightness" in the direction that your life is headed. There will often be a smile on your face when these parts of you team up and contribute their skills together each day.

When Intention Power and Expression Power are out of balance, blocked, or diminished: Your clarity of what you are doing will be impacted because there will be a sense of futility and boredom with your daily life. You'll find yourself dragging through your chores, assignments, and responsibilities with a feeling of resignation. You may find that you rely on stimulants, diversions, and distractions to get you through your day. The only reward is simply the paycheck. You'll feel that something is missing in your day and you wish you could find a way to feel more engaged with your personal talents and interests.

Pursuing your life intentions is intended to be inspiring and fulfilling while consistently providing direction for your life. It connects you to your authentic truth. Ideally, you are aware of who you are and convey that understanding to everyone you meet. The biggest obstacle to your authenticity is wearing a mask for the sake of gaining approval, popularity, or likability from those you want to impress at the expense of your authenticity.

What if you could simply say, "This is who I am. This is my life assignment direction, should I choose to accept it." Wouldn't that be satisfying? You would then find true friends and colleagues who would appreciate and support who you are and why you are here.

Intention Power meets Intimacy Power

You're meant to support your life intentions by living authentically and taking care of your daily needs. When you're nurturing your Intimacy and Intention Power needs, your body keeps on supporting you without complaint. Your heart is open, strong, and willing to be vulnerable. All your personal relationships are ideally feeding these two aspects of your personality. When you find those kinds of connections, you will feel gratitude and upliftment in being with your close friends and significant partners.

When Intention Power and Intimacy Power are balanced: You are following your dreams and feeling internally satisfied, filled with love and mutual support. There will be a natural synergistic dance between your Intention and Intimacy Powers, allowing for inner contentment and overall life satisfaction. You'll go through your life with a smile on your face and a warmth that emanates from a huggable nature. As you support each of these two personality aspects, you enrich your life with internal harmony and will find new ways to keep energizing your future.

When Intention Power and Intimacy Power are out of balance, blocked, or diminished: You feel heavy inside and unsupported, though some form of stress is weighing you down and inhibiting you from continuing down your ideal life path. You'll also likely feel alone or disheartened, as you have few opportunities to share yourself with others in an intimate or intentionally close manner. This is why it is essential to fulfill your personal Intimacy Power needs and start sharing yourself and your Intention Power dreams with others. When you find a special friendship that aligns with your personal visions, hold on and enjoy the ride. Your Intimacy and Intention pairing brings happiness and true love into your life.

Do you remember the courage of that little five-year-old boy who was part of our Kinder Colors program (Chapter 1)? He proclaimed, "I am a Super Hugger, and that's who I am." Wouldn't it be wonderful if you had that kind of courage to express and live out your authentic Powers and gifts every day? When you do that, there's no second-guessing, no insecurity, no need to impress; there's simply truth, communication, and clear action. This is the kind of relationship you want to cultivate and easily embrace in your life as you follow your intentions.

Intention Power meets Life Force Power

My favorite collaboration is the harmonious union of your Life Force and Intention Powers. Your Life Force Power captain/pitcher sends the ball to your Intention Power catcher, and together they orchestrate the main dynamics of your life play. When you lose this interplay, the game of life is put on hold. Your life goals and passions fuel your direction and purpose. There will always be a collaboration that makes this duo essential and integral to everything you do.

When Intention Power and Life Force Power are balanced: You passionately and eagerly embrace a growth mindset, always looking forward to what's next with zest and excitement. These two aspects of your personality must have a harmonious relationship. You pretty much start your day with that first burst of Life Force Power energy and the Intention Power, catching the first breath in the morning. What are you getting up for today, and what do you want to experience or accomplish? These two aspects guide your entire Vibrancy Signature team and provide the anchor of your life experiences.

When Intention Power and Life Force Power are out of balance, blocked, or diminished: Your energy and inner motivation are suppressed, making challenges feel impossible and the future seem frightening or out of reach. You might lose the will to live and see no real purpose in your life. You feel detached from everything, and the game of life is paused, like a rain delay. The sunlight needs to return to help dry your field of depression and give you a chance to rediscover your spark of hope and purpose.

How Your Intention Power Impacts Your Psychological Health

- Enables you to live life with direction and purpose
- Provides a focus and intent for your day
- Keeps you sensitive to your personality needs
- Enhances your willingness to compromise and negotiate with others

- Nourishes your dreams and higher goals
- Connects with your imagination and future

You should always listen to your inner music and remember your personal theme song. It's like the fabric that weaves through everything you think, feel, and do. For me, it's my colorful Violet Intention Power with the Power of Hope that plays in the background of my life's journey. In my early years, there were many occasions when my hope for the future was dashed and I felt lost. These experiences were accompanied by a devastatingly bleak outlook and an inability to see beyond my grief and sorrow. Anytime there was a death or a relationship ending in my life, it was very difficult for me to see a bright future ahead.

Once I began to consciously understand this aspect of my Vibrancy Signature, I was able to step beyond distractions, tragic events, and disappointments and maintain a hopeful outlook regardless of the circumstances. It required a significant amount of personal internal healing to accept this aspect of my personality.

Each day, I now know to infuse my being with a hopeful perspective and a clear vision of my future. I finally feel free to catch every ball of life from a hope-filled vantage point rather than be tempted down that old worn-out road to negativity, despair, and hopelessness.

Chaya's Primary Intention Power: Enthusiasm (Blue Green)

This time, instead of sharing a story about myself, I'm sharing one about my wife's Intention Power, to illustrate how profound shifts in your relationship can occur when you understand your partner's Vibrancy Signature.

Shortly after Chaya and I were married, she was enthusiastically telling me a story from her day while we prepared dinner in the kitchen of our first home. I briefly interrupted her to express how incredible it was to be on the receiving end of her enthusiasm. At first, she thought I was telling her to calm down or chill out, as she had been told so many times before. Instead, I affirmed her Intention Power of Enthusiasm (Blue Green) as her amazing superpower. I told her that I loved how excited, enthused, and full of life she was. She laughed and said that it was the first time anyone had interrupted her to validate her naturally exuberant nature. If she ever stops being her true self, consistently expressing her "yippy yahoo" essence, she risks slipping into melancholy and sadness.

This illustrates the importance of fully embracing your Intention Power and allowing it to saturate your life with its music, inspiring all your Powers to play ball.

How Your Intention Power Impacts Your Physical Health

- Supports your tissue health in every body system
- Fuels your cerebrospinal flow connections
- Maintains your neurological sensitivity
- Inspires your mind–body awareness
- Promotes your cellular communication
- Heightens your energy field awareness

> Your Intention Power is the energy that flows through your body tissues. When you're following your life intentions, your body is humming with pleasure.

Your body tissues are like the theme song behind what you're feeling and thinking in your life. Every cell of your body is whispering its story. Your Intention Power is the energy that flows through your body tissues. When you're following your life intentions, your body is humming with pleasure.

Any breakdown in your skin, connective tissue, other organs, glands, or bones is related to a stress that has been resonating for too long inside your body. When you decide to clear that stress, the song of your life is more easily heard. It's never easy to change your life path. But you can reinvent yourself and upgrade your theme song to one that nourishes your future and enlivens your present.

One way to determine whether you're following your Intention Power and the path to happiness is to observe how well your body tissues are held together and nourished. The health of your tissues and cellular communication radiantly broadcasts instantaneously throughout your body.

The Intention Power in Action: Sylvia's Story

It's so easy to be thrown off your life path by others' unsolicited comments, critiques, or judgments of what they think you should do with your life. One of my clients, Sylvia, requested a Vibrancy Signature coaching session shortly after she turned 65 to explore her potential retirement options.

Sylvia began tearing up in her session immediately after receiving validation for her personal career talents. For the first time, she said, she really understood what motivated her and how she most easily found satisfaction in her daily life, particularly from her work. She shared how she loved her job, and even though her friends urged her to retire, she honestly didn't want to, but felt pressured by them to move on. She discovered that her job seemed to nourish all her Primary Vibrancy Signature strengths, and of course she didn't want to let herself go and abandon something she loved.

Her job was a perfect fit for what she felt was her life direction and specifically supported her Intention Power. So after our session, Sylvia decided to turn the day-to-day operations of her job over to a long-term colleague but to stay on in an advisory role so she could participate in the company whenever she chose. This way, she could continue to do what she loved whenever she liked and keep actively engaged with other activities that were equally nourishing and uplifting for this next phase of her life.

Wrapping It All Up: The Intention Power

Are you being true to yourself right now? When you learn to say no to situations and people who don't understand you, you ultimately create space to say yes to what you truly prefer and who you want to share your life with. Pleasing others is noble, but not at the expense of your own happiness or wellbeing. Your Intention Power is the song on your lips, creating harmony and a smooth cadence in your life.

You deserve a life filled with joy in all your relationships, including work, chores, recreation, service, and play. This is how you begin to live authentically and with congruence in your life. When you present your true self, you feel strong, alive, and purposeful. If you suppress these qualities, you will experience pain, suffering, and despair. You may feel the loss of yourself and miss the connections that are only possible when you are true to your inner nature. This is how your Intention Power guides you on your path to balance and peace.

*   *   *

This completes the overview of the five aspects of your Primary Vibrancy Signature. Keep in mind that these five Vibrancy Powers—Environment, Expression, Intimacy, Life Force, and Intention—overlap within you, leading to natural competition within your personality at different times throughout your life. You'll ultimately find that your happiest moments occur when each aspect of your personality gets to play its music and express its unique talents every day. Your task is to familiarize yourself with your Vibrancy Signature Powers, getting to know them individually and as a team working together. This is like having an owner's manual to guide you throughout your life.

PART THREE

Opening up to a Colorful Future

What's Possible After Discovering Your Vibrancy Signature

CHAPTER 10

Healing from the Inside Out

Each of your Vibrancy Signature Powers is a key to your lifelong health and happiness. Once you understand the basics, it's time to begin embracing your own self-discovery a bit more deeply.

Learning How to Embrace Your Potential and Find Balance

It all starts with honoring the gifts of your Vibrancy Powers. Many of my clients initially have a difficult time seeing the positive characteristics of their five Primary Vibrancy Signature Powers. Think of a five-cylinder engine that runs smoothly, but as soon as one of those cylinders stops firing, there is reduced power, rough idling, and engine misfiring. It's very common to grow up in environments that do not support your Vibrancy Signature Power needs.

When this happens, you'll attempt to protect yourself by shutting down or escaping what feels like an unsupportive environment.

This marks the beginning of you leaving the truly healthy wiring of your Vibrancy Signature. To ensure you *don't* do this, you must learn how to recognize either your excessive or contracted shadow adaptations and correct them accordingly.

Here's what I mean by that: If you feel like someone doesn't really get you, there may be times when you try extra hard to prove your worth. This comes with the cost of an underlying insecurity and exhaustion from trying to convince others you are worthy of their love, respect, or caring. This is the excessive shadow stress that causes you to live in a hyper-aggressive mindset, always trying to prove yourself but never feeling good enough inside. Alternatively, there is the contracted shadow coping mechanism, where you run away from your true Vibrancy Power gifts.

Suppressing your true nature carries a heavy cost. You try to please others by acting in ways you believe they expect from you. As a result, your self-esteem and confidence shrink or you overcompensate with hyper-productivity. In either case, you're left feeling empty or burned out just trying to be yourself.

Once you identify your shadow adaptations, you can begin to self-regulate and pull yourself back to the center of your own life. It is also very helpful to have people in your life who are fully aware of this dynamic and can continue to hold up a mirror to your natural strengths and abilities, and your true potential. Your balanced, healthy nature will start to show up more and more when you are seen and acknowledged, and when you begin to positively affirm your own Vibrancy Powers.

Being yourself should be like breathing—easy, effortless, and no big deal. Unfortunately, around 75% of my clients initially have at least one of their Primary Vibrancy Signature Powers in either a contracted or expansive state.

> Once you identify your shadow adaptations, you can begin to self-regulate and pull yourself back to the center of your own life.

When you can have a conversation that helps you learn to embrace your potential, your life gets a reboot, and your five-cylinder engine begins to purr.

Reinforcing your Primary Vibrancy Signature Powers is something you can do repeatedly. My clients often tell me they review their Vibrancy Signature information annually or more frequently. Additionally, your discovery process can continue to mature as you learn to embrace yourself more each day. When you accept yourself fully, you begin to find your path of harmony and vitality.

Nobody shows up fully in life if they are discounted, ignored, or devalued. Think of a world-class musician playing in a subway for rushing commuters. Most ignore this "unfortunate" person's predicament. But those who slow down to appreciate the music and pay attention to its creator are rewarded with an exceptionally beautiful experience.

Similarly, you must grace your Vibrancy Powers with your attention and learn to see them as the unique gifts they are. You can then start sharing yourself from that vantage point.

Your Personal and Career Needs Are Unique

In your Primary Vibrancy Signature, you have Environment, Life Force, and Intention Powers that uniquely calibrate with your Intimacy and Expression Powers. Your Expression Power is wired to share your gifts and talents, and it drives your desire to contribute to the world. Meanwhile, your Intimacy Power supports you in creating closeness, warmth, connection, and the fulfillment of your personal needs and desires. These are the yin and yang of your personality, which must always be kept in balance for you to have a healthy and fulfilling life. While these two aspects are distinct, they both share a common need for certain types of surroundings (your Environment Power), life motivations (your Life Force Power), and personal goals and life direction (your Intention Power).

The key to finding your own life path is to follow your vibrancy gifts and talents. To do this, you must be aware of what your Intimacy and Expression Powers have as gifts and natural abilities. Whenever you're exploring your next life path and future, you should clearly distinguish between your Expression Power and your Intimacy Power. I have seen many clients choose college majors, careers, and vocations that don't fully align with their Expression Power, and this doesn't serve them well in the long run. How many people do you know who feel dissatisfied, burned out, or bored with what they do for a living? After years of studying, training, and incurring expenses, most people will just "suck it up" and continue living this subpar life. That is, until their physical, emotional, or mental health breaks down and they get in touch with their real self.

Your ideal livelihood will keep you young. It will never be boring if you listen to and follow your Vibrancy Power strengths. However, since your Vibrancy Signature owner's manual for life was not readily available, you most likely tried to do your best, adopting a win some, lose some attitude toward the jobs you've had in your life.

Once you're clear about the gifts your Vibrancy Expression Power offers, you'll design your life around those skills that are yours to play with and serve the world as you desire. When you do this in your unique way, the world is grateful and will offer financial support, gratitude, and appreciation. Along the way, you'll feel a sense of value, satisfaction, and contentment that comes from doing what you love.

When you truly support yourself, it makes you happy and also serves as a perfect example for those around you. Everyone wants to have a full and enjoyable life. But most folks are caught in their shadow stress and don't know how to extricate themselves from their own pain and unhappiness. Once your Expression Power is doing its thing, it gives you the ability to search for your personal Intimacy Power balance in your life.

You deserve to be cherished for who you are. Your true friends and family will understand and appreciate your unique Vibrancy Intimacy Power. If they don't, then they are not seeing who you really are. It is your job to introduce them to the real you.

Finding Your Way Through Social and Cultural Pressures

We all grow up with families who, in some way, expect us to meet their expectations. When you only follow others' expectations, it might seem like it pleases them, but it can also make you miserable. The best thing you can do is respect their choices and ask them to honor your preferences. They may not at first. But when they see how happy you are by being your authentic self, most of the time they'll come around.

All relationships have expectations—some are reasonable, some are toxic, some make your life great, and others create stress and obligation. The more you live in alignment with your Vibrancy Powers, the easier it becomes to clearly identify the relationship expectations that work for you and those you'd prefer to negotiate or change.

> The more you live in alignment with your Vibrancy Powers, the easier it becomes to clearly identify the relationship expectations that work for you and those you'd prefer to negotiate or change.

For example, if your family wants you to pursue a career that has nothing to do with your Expression Power, let them know that it is not your ideal strength. You must then show them your real talents, gifts, and unique Vibrancy Expression superpower. The more you can gradually share your full Vibrancy Signature with your family, the easier it will be to negotiate these expectations and find ways to mutually support, love, and respect one another's choices in life.

We live in a world that has a variety of social norms. These norms are created to encourage people to be kind, supportive, and helpful to one another. However, sometimes social norms are contrary to your personal Vibrancy Signature. For example, if you grow up in a society that wants you to be serious, attentive, and follow in the footsteps of your elders, this could be wonderful or awful depending upon your unique Vibrancy Signature Powers. If you have the Power of Laughter (Lemon), you will gag at seriousness because you want to be a comedian. When you have the Power of Authenticity (Lavender), you'll desire to follow your heart and strongly resist any societal rules for your lifestyle. Or if you have the Power of Leadership (Nectarine), you'll want to carve out your own path and make your own decisions about what you do and don't do.

Whenever you're trapped in cultural stereotypes that don't align with your Vibrancy Signature Powers, you'll feel out of sorts and uncomfortable. For instance, I taught a class in Switzerland many years ago and was told that my students, based on cultural expectations, would be very serious and studious. In one of my Vibrancy Signature lessons, we were learning about the Power of Energizing (Saffron), which we affectionately call the "loving butt-kicker." To demonstrate, we formed a circle and proceeded to demonstrate this silly descriptive term. My "serious" students demonstrated that they could be silly, playful, and irreverent in that little demonstration.

I have clients worldwide. In every country I visit, there are certain cultural traditions, norms, and beliefs, but humanity is still humanity. You get to be your authentic self. Each of your colorful Vibrancy Signature Powers is distinctive, regardless of your skin color, ethnic background, cultural heritage, or social class. This is what makes you special and gives you a unique human perspective and personality. There is no one just like you, regardless of your heritage or upbringing. Your Vibrancy Signature is your true genetic birth descriptor.

Interpersonal Relationships

Your Vibrancy Signature is tied to your genetic family patterns. I have seen many generations of extended family members who have the same Vibrancy Powers. This can be helpful in some cases, because a natural rapport is established with people who share the same Vibrancy Powers. However, if any of these family members are living in the shadow of their true selves, it will be even more difficult for you to live in your colorful nature. This is because you are subtly expected to shut yourself off from your own inner light by following in their stress-filled shoes.

In many family dynamics, I've also seen that a person who possesses Vibrancy Powers that are not shared by other family members is often considered the rebel or "black sheep" of the family. This is why it's so important to break the prejudice, stereotypes, and lack of understanding and replace them with a deeper, more accurate view of our humanity and energetic wiring that the Vibrancy Signature provides.

The harmony and compatibility of your relationships depend on how successfully you mutually live according to your own Vibrancy Power gifts.

Molding your partner to fit your needs likely shows you don't truly appreciate who they are. It's analogous to trying to convince a trombone player to play the violin. You have unique personality "instruments" and talents to share, just as your partner does. When you build relationships on this inner truth, you're more likely to experience compatibility, mutual understanding, and personal growth. Your Vibrancy Powers will never change, but they will blossom and flourish as your ease of being evolves and matures over time.

In other words, you can create your future by "rebooting" your deeper soul-filled perspective of who you really are inside.

> The harmony and compatibility of your relationships depend on how successfully you mutually live according to your own Vibrancy Power gifts.

This is how I began this journey back in the early 1980s. I got to discover the wireless anatomy of the human body and how the soul steps into this physical vehicle we drive around in. When you look at your relationships from this vantage point, it's all about reverence and appreciation. This is why I see my clients as works of art, regardless of where they are in their growth and healing processes.

You are entirely original and beautifully vibrant. When you are recognized for your Vibrancy Powers instead of your pathology or weaknesses, it strongly boosts your sense of self. That's why people enjoy discovering this deeper view of themselves.

As you foster a life in which you really live your truth, you'll never forget when you first discovered your Vibrancy Signature. I have clients who, decades later, tell me their lives changed on that day. When you know yourself, you are happy. When you are seen deeply at a soul level, you feel loved. When your personality quirks are viewed as gifts, you relax and enjoy your life. There is never any judgment or need to fix yourself, just a chance to step into living your best self each day. And you will gravitate toward people and communities that appreciate and honor your light-filled personality and welcome you wholeheartedly.

Your Primary Vibrancy Signature is the blueprint of your inner and outer beauty and greatness. Get ready to shine your light to the world.

CHAPTER 11

Building Bridges to Others

What if you truly could see people for who they really are from the inside? Knowing a person's Vibrancy Signature gives you a clear glimpse of their human potential and what makes them feel seen, loved, and understood. Using this powerful tool in your relationships is valuable in both personal and professional settings. It enhances your self-awareness, improves relationship compatibility, fosters effective communication, and builds easy rapport. When you understand someone's Vibrancy Signature, you are perceiving their innate energetic state and how they are most authentically themselves. This can enhance deeper empathy and connection, as you can support them in living in alignment with their truest self.

This is why this tool of understanding can transform not just your own life, but all your significant relationships, and the evolution of our society and culture. It helps you gain insight into the unique ways individuals experience and interact with the world.

By having a deep understanding of others' personality traits, you can step into their world and make an immediate difference in their life.

> By having a deep understanding of others' personality traits, you can step into their world and make an immediate difference in their life.

In the process, you build better relationships all around that support personal growth and create more fulfillment for all.

When I developed this system, it became apparent to me that knowing the Vibrancy Signatures of every single one of my clients, coworkers, family members, and anyone I cared for would give both them and me fresh and life-changing insights and understanding about them. In fact, at a certain point in time, I felt I was doing my clients a disservice if I gave them a specific recommendation without first knowing their Vibrancy Signature. Once I understood who they were and what they truly needed, it helped solidify the bridge of understanding and healing that I was committed to cultivating for my clients. This is possible across the board in our human life experience.

Understanding Your Family

Once I understood all the members of my family from their unique Vibrancy Signatures, it helped me forgive, value, and appreciate them even more. Growing up in a family where, as a child, you expect everyone to give you what you need to feel loved and supported every day can be challenging. When this doesn't happen, you may see them as cruel, unloving, or lacking in some way. In some ways, you are being raised in an environment where, at times, each of you is speaking a different language. Once you understand your family members from this Vibrancy Signature perspective, it begins to soften your "inner child" complaints and wounds, helping you expand your tolerance and appreciation.

As I mentioned earlier, there are hereditary patterns in your family Vibrancy Powers. In my case, I inherited one of mine from each of my parents. I also share two other Vibrancy Powers with a few of my siblings. This provided some natural rapport and understanding with each of them. However, when you expect your family to get you and they don't for a variety of reasons, it can be painful. As the youngest of eight children in a large extended family, I got to experience their challenges, their wounds, and their needs and often felt invisible myself. For me, that pain diminished greatly as an adult when I finally stepped into their shoes with empathy for their own personal needs. Now I can accept and value them for who they are, not for what my younger self needed them to be.

Understanding Your Classmates' Differences

As you grow up and start making friends, it becomes immediately clear that you are very different from your classmates. What if you could participate in your own version of a Kinder Colors program and be seen and valued by others right away? This would make all the difference scholastically, socially, and personally as you begin to see your value and understand what makes you and your classmates special. You might also be known as the Super Hugger, the

Super Leader, the Super Supporter, or the Super Learner. When teachers have this universal language of humanity at their fingertips, it greatly enhances their ability to reach each child in their own unique way.

By learning about the positive Vibrancy Power characteristics that are inherent in each of us, it becomes easier to see when those qualities are not showing up. Instead of reacting, rejecting, or avoiding a classmate who is displaying a disruptive or confusing behavior, we can offer compassion, support, and comfort and remember who they are beneath the surface. We know that whenever we go down the shadow road of our Vibrancy Powers, we are deeply in pain and temporarily lost. What a wonderful opportunity to eliminate judgment, defensiveness, and cruelty toward others when they are suffering inside. This tool can help you recognize your classmates' differences and understand how to connect with them effectively using a new language of empathy and appreciation.

Aligning Your Ideal Relationships

Someday, I imagine a world where any new relationship begins with the question "What are your Colorful Powers?" (Remember, with the Power of Hope (Violet) in my Vibrancy Signature, I am always dreaming of what I'd like to see in the world.) Many of my clients over the years have started their new relationships by ensuring they are in alignment with their respective Vibrancy Signatures. Every Vibrancy Power has specific strengths and preferences. Can you imagine that the needs of the Power of Energizing (Saffron) are very different from the needs of the Power of Relaxation (Mocha)? If you've ever seen a photograph of a colorful tent pitched high on the side of a mountain, this is an example of these two Vibrancy Powers combining, with intense, energetic climbing immediately followed by deep, relaxing recovery. This is a great metaphor for what is possible in a relationship, regardless of the Powers involved.

Understanding other people's personalities allows you to better respond to their needs, anticipate reactions, and build stronger connections. It helps in recognizing different communication styles, emotional triggers, and preferences, leading to fewer conflicts and more harmonious interactions in personal relationships and friendships.

If you can grasp and appreciate another person and what makes them special, you are halfway there to building a great relationship. Too often, our personal biases get in the way of attempting to find an ideal connection. We may bring just the "energetic medicine" or Vibrancy Powers that the other person craves.

> Understanding other people's personalities allows you to better respond to their needs, anticipate reactions, and build stronger connections.

My wife and I don't share any Colorful Vibrancy Powers, but because we understand each other and value each other's gifts, we have created the foundation for an ideal relationship. With your new language of Vibrancy Powers, you can avoid losing yourself in a codependent, weak relationship dynamic. Instead, you'll be empowered to find a way to harmonize your differences, just as people singing together in a duet can learn to do.

Over the years, one of my favorite moments is when I talk to a couple who just discovered each other's Vibrancy Signature Powers and began their relationship anew even though they have been married for decades. They often find that the Vibrancy Signature experience helps them develop more closeness and understanding almost instantly. When you understand your partner's underlying personality traits that may have contributed to a conflict, you can approach it with more empathy and find solutions that address the core issues. Instead of being critical of each other, there is understanding. Instead of trying to change each other's behavior, there is encouragement to find outlets for each one's particular unmet needs.

All it takes is a new paradigm of personality awareness to catalyze a turn toward the ideal of relationship harmony. You can read a dozen relationship how-to self-help books, and they would not come close to having the same insights as discovering your partner's Vibrancy Signature.

Building Bridges in Action: Creating Mutually Supportive Environments

I once worked with a married couple that had very different Environment Powers. The wife had the Power of Intuition (Indigo), with a desire to be in nature, while the husband had the Power of Connecting (Indigo Topaz) as his, valuing social connections with friends and family. As you can imagine, this situation caused considerable tension and discord for them…until we discovered a simple solution. Their favorite getaway was a cabin in northern Minnesota, where she could listen to loons calling across the lake, and he could occasionally invite his family and friends to join them. Both had their needs met, and they began to understand each other effortlessly.

This is the key to any good relationship. By first understanding your innate needs and then discussing them, you can create a win-win scenario with just a bit of creative effort and flexibility.

Networking with Colleagues

Knowing the Vibrancy Signatures of the people you work with—including those from other countries and diverse lifestyles—can help you quickly create a powerful and functional personal and professional network. Recognizing how different personalities process information and make decisions can significantly improve communication.

It's been affirming for me to see my long-standing clients and colleagues in the Vibrancy Path Community come together and have instant rapport with one another when they know each other's Colorful Powers. Because they speak a language of appreciating differences and respecting each other's innate gifts, I've witnessed how such a community of people can more easily grow, develop, and work together without being divided by politics, religion, social status, or any other personal bias. They tend to come willing to embrace the human spectrum of Vibrancy Powers and are genuinely curious about how that shows up in others in the group.

In addition to benefiting from our differences, there is also a lot of joy and comfort in having certain Vibrancy Powers in the room. When you realize that you share the same Vibrancy Power with another person, you'll naturally feel an instant connection as though they are a long-lost friend. Likewise, if you are "in the market" for a particular Vibrancy Power such as stability, love, or understanding, you'll be grateful that someone with that Power shows up just when you need them.

Bringing the wisdom of the Vibrancy Signature into your workplace provides numerous valuable opportunities to learn from the embodiment of these Colorful Vibrancy Powers as they shine in living color within your group dynamics in real time. You can learn to cherish and network with people in a whole new light of understanding. Building this type of relationship is far more genuine. You never have to try to impress with your background, status, or position. You simply say what your Vibrancy Signature Powers are—and you are seen and known right away. This can foster true relationship harmony, appreciation, and functional interactions.

Effectively Support Your Clients

By understanding what truly energizes and fulfills someone, you can better support their wellbeing, encourage them in pursuits that align with their purpose, and help them cultivate a more vibrant life. Looking at your client's or patient's Vibrancy Signature takes your personal bias out of the equation, and you simply step into their needs and craft a healing path designed just for them.

Can you imagine what it would be like if every therapist, doctor, coach, and healing practitioner had access to your Vibrancy Signature blueprint? You would no longer feel unseen or misunderstood, or receive advice that contradicts what you know you really need. Plus, you can save yourself a lot of time and frustration that would otherwise be spent trying to explain who you are. It takes the complication and struggles out of not getting someone's real problem or true need. Once you step into their world, each client will think that you are magical because you really understand them and their concerns. But it only seems magical because most people haven't considered it possible to identify a person's core makeup and needs with such accuracy. Often, there is a disconnect because the real issues are being ignored in favor of the practitioner's newest technique, treatment plan, pill, or frankly, personal bias. When you see a person for who they are on all levels of their being, you can immediately become more effective as a listener, healer, and empathic person. This then grounds your personal healing experience with greater human depth and soul wisdom.

No matter how complicated the psychological or physical problem is, there is always a way to unwind the stress by getting to the core of the client's authentic needs that were not being met. Every person has their own specific path of healing, and when you understand their Vibrancy Signature, you can help remind them of their own life path journey.

Build Functional Organizations and Teams

In a professional setting, understanding diverse personalities within a team can lead to better collaboration, delegation, and conflict resolution. Much disharmony and organizational chaos stem from team members not being willing to see the true potential in each person's personality gifts or understanding what they need to effectively thrive. Each person brings their unique Colorful Vibrancy Power strengths, and recognizing these can create a well-rounded, productive environment.

If you are committed to building an organization that emphasizes personal growth, human understanding, and self-realization, then you are in the right place. The Vibrancy Path is made up of a community of leaders who are at the leading edge of personal transformation and regenerative healing philosophy. From this perspective, your business or organization can expand your effectiveness and step into a new paradigm of team-building excellence.

> The Vibrancy Path is made up of a community of leaders who are at the leading edge of personal transformation and regenerative healing philosophy.

When you bring your awareness of the Vibrancy Signature to your professional organization or team, you'll immediately notice improved harmony and communication, more creative solutions, and a success mindset that infuses everyone. When each member gets to offer their strengths, be appreciated for their unique talents, and never feel undervalued, there is a transformative shift in the organization. Every person is bringing their A game to the team because, by being seen for their true Vibrancy Signature value, they are naturally inclined to let those parts of their nature shine fully and contribute freely. By adopting this enlightened perspective, you can establish a win-win strategy for every member of the organization and utilize their contributions to amplify the impact of your work in the world.

A Template for True Social Harmony

The Vibrancy Path is focused on understanding differences. It is not just theoretical but rather a window into the "play of consciousness" and how that can lead to positive relationships both locally and globally. This play of life described by philosophers, sages, and visionaries is where you can find your true mission and purpose and begin contributing to enlightening the world around you. As you step into your Vibrancy Signature and start expressing your authentic Vibrancy Powers, a change will occur—first within yourself, and then in the community around you.

Imagine a movement in education to evaluate the Vibrancy Signatures of every kindergartner. How would that impact the lives of those children? To be seen and valued for their superpowers at such a formative age would have a lasting impact on their lives. Likewise, if teachers were given the chance to take a summer course in setting up a Vibrancy Signature classroom, they could create a learning environment of appreciation and tailored support for students much more effectively. These visions simply need a little fertilization and support to become a reality.

Take this further and imagine improvements in society where there is always a core value placed on the people involved and their true needs and where social concerns are simply rooted in which Vibrancy Powers you bring to others in your world. Do you bring the Power of Compassion (White), Leadership (Nectarine), Laughter (Lemon), or some other unique powerful contribution?

Whenever a person acts in an antisocial way, they are simply acting out the shadow of not being seen for their true Vibrancy Power gifts. You can see people struggling in this world and the lack of harmony. Prejudices, judgment, bigotry, and hatred are the antithesis of the Vibrancy Path philosophy. Our world will achieve social harmony only when we can learn to appreciate what each of us brings to our pursuit of happiness and belonging. The moment you feel at peace is linked with being seen, appreciated, valued, and understood. These are the primary ingredients of the Vibrancy Path.

No matter how lost you sometimes feel, there is a way through the darkness by seeing and radiating your own true light. That is why learning a language that sees the unique rainbow Vibrancy Signature of each person gives hope for our future and helps us dream of a world where we can fully appreciate each other. I have studied many social programs around the world, and the most successful give each person a positive reflection of their abilities and self-worth. Once you believe in your own value, life can change for you and for everyone you interact with. And if you can help people discover a language of their true value, gifts, and innate superpowers, they can wake up to their inherent worth and begin to transform!

The social harmony everyone craves becomes possible one person at a time.

Uncovering your Vibrancy Signature Powers is the first step in awakening your world from a pathological view of people's problems to an enlightened perspective of human potential.

CHAPTER 12

Your Inner Vibrancy Signature

Take Yourself to the Next Level

When you first learn about the five aspects of your Primary Vibrancy Signature, it's exciting, validating, and extremely eye-opening. These are the foundational Powers that help you activate your unique expression and gifts in the world. Let's do a quick recap of these five core Vibrancy Signature Powers and their distinct jobs.

The first three physical aspects are in charge of very specific facets of your life.

- **Your Environment Power** designates both a contribution you bring to all environments and what you need within those environments to thrive.

- **Your Expression Power** signifies what you need to bring into your career and hobbies to feel fulfilled and purposeful in your contributions.

- **Your Intimacy Power** enriches your personal time and helps determine what you need in relationships to feel loved and open your heart to others.

The last two physical aspects, each in their own way, have a profound impact on all your Vibrancy Signature team members.

- **Your Life Force Power** is a central theme and the driving force in your life, providing abundant energy for all your endeavors.

- **Your Intention Power** describes the style in which you live your life and serves as the backdrop or theme song for everything you do.

However, this is only the beginning of uncovering your incredible personality blueprint. Nine additional aspects make up what I call your Inner Vibrancy Signature.

Introducing the Three Inner Aspects of Your Vibrancy Signature— Emotional, Communication, and Mental

Springing from each of the first three aspects of your Vibrancy Signature (Environment, Expression, and Intimacy) are three additional dimensions that provide a deeper layer of understanding your nature: emotional, communication, and mental. These nine total aspects outline the emotional, communicative, and cognitive personality aptitudes and talents with respect to your Environment, Expression, and Intimacy vibrational nature. These develop early in your life and continue to impact you throughout your life.

> Your Inner Vibrancy Signature continues your unique developmental journey into the realm of what best supports you to stay emotionally stable, communicate with ease, and think clearly.

Your Inner Vibrancy Signature continues your unique developmental journey into the realm of what best supports you to stay emotionally stable, communicate with ease, and think clearly.

Emotional Powers

Each of the three Emotional Powers in your Inner Vibrancy Signature (Emotional Environment Power, Emotional Expression Power, and Emotional Intimacy Power) plays a role in how you experience emotional sustenance and energy. Whenever you feel distraught or empty inside, these three emotional aspects of your Vibrancy Signature are out of balance and need support. This support might come from a gentle touch, an eye gaze, a laugh, a smile, or simply a deep connection with your body. These fundamental emotional needs create the foundation for your emotional thriving and grounding for the rest of your life.

Communication Powers

Your unique communication nature serves as the internal bridge connecting your emotional and mental aspects. Every feeling and thought you experience can be expressed and articulated through your Communication Power trio (Communication Environment Power, Communication Expression Power, and Communication Intimacy Power). Your Communication Powers are invaluable members of your Vibrancy Signature team. Your spoken words and internal dialogue influence your thoughts and feelings, which in turn shape your reality.

Mental Powers

Your trio of Inner Mental Powers (Mental Environment Power, Mental Expression Power, and Mental Intimacy Power) defines how you stay mentally sharp, clear-headed, and brimming with great ideas. After all, you are what you think, and these facets of your personality influence your overall mental health. When your Mental Powers function in a balanced and uplifting manner, you'll easily navigate your daily experiences. However, when you experience mental discord and confusion in any of your three Mental Powers, you'll temporarily lose the ability to orchestrate your life with clarity and precision.

The Magic of Your Vibrancy Signature

Each of your Vibrancy Signature Powers (the five Primary Physical Powers and the nine Inner Powers) influences different facets of your daily life. None are expendable or less important. I frequently get asked "What is my main Power?" All 14 are your main Powers!

The more you're conscious of these dynamics inside your personality, the more enlivened you become. It's like any collaborative group of musicians, artists, or friends who really get each other and complement one another. By following your heart and listening to your inner life calling, you'll move more in alignment with your authentic nature. Ideally, you then attract people doing the same thing, and you can each share in your creatively unique and engaging way. The key is bringing your whole psyche to the table, not just one facet of your personality. This is the artistic dance of getting to know your entire Vibrancy Signature team—a powerful ensemble of 14 Vibrancy Powers working for you 24/7.

Ultimately, it's all about finding your audience—people and a niche that nourishes you and allows you to shine. Imagine being wired to be a comedian yet never having the chance to perform your stand-up routine. Or consider if you're called to be a natural leader but have only found yourself in supporting roles. This is why—for your personal vitality, sanity, and "joy meter"—you must play the parts you were meant to embody. Keep this in mind as you engage with others. It's common to create unflattering labels, to box people into limitations, or to misjudge their natural abilities. When this happens to you, it can be painful, disconcerting, and disheartening.

Get to know your Vibrancy Signature first, and then get curious about how the people in your world are wired to be their unique selves as well.

> Get to know your Vibrancy Signature first, and then get curious about how the people in your world are wired to be their unique selves as well.

Like a conductor, your job is to bring these instruments of your personality together and help them produce beautiful music. You're on an amazing journey of self-discovery. Deep inside you is a soul that wants to wake up to your life purpose, activate your talents, and ignite your reason for being. You're here to understand, appreciate, and embrace the light-filled Powers that animate your body, emotions, communicative nature, and mind. This is the intention of the Vibrancy Path, and it is my privilege to witness others as they discover their Vibrancy Signature Powers and begin a journey to embrace each one.

You're here to design your life with congruency and follow your inner voice of who you were meant to be.

This is your special life opportunity, and it's up to you to leave your signature on it!

ABOUT THE AUTHOR

Jamie Champion is a visionary educator and developer of the Vibrancy Signature system—an approach to understanding how our individual energy patterns influence physical health, emotional resilience, mental clarity, and overall life fulfillment. With a deep passion for helping others awaken their full energetic potential, Jamie has spent over four decades immersed in holistic wellness, vibrational healing, and personal transformation. He bridges ancient energetic principles with contemporary insights from neuroscience, somatic healing, and psychology.

As the creator of the Vibrancy Path and the Vibrancy Signature frameworks, Jamie helps individuals discover their unique energetic blueprint—what makes them feel most alive, authentic, and aligned with their true nature. His approach empowers people to shift from confusion and depletion into clarity, vitality, and purpose. He has developed tools that support nervous system balance, authentic self-expression, and sustainable wellbeing.

Known for his gentle clarity, intuitive insight, and grounded teaching style, Jamie offers guidance that is both practical and soul-nourishing. Through retreats, workshops, online classes, and private sessions, he has supported thousands of people in reconnecting with their core vibrancy and creating more fulfilling lives.

Jamie lives in the Blue Ridge Mountains of central Virginia, where he, his wife Chaya, and their "fur family" find inspiration in the rhythms of nature, meaningful conversations, personal growth and healing, and quiet moments of reflection.

GLOSSARY

Ayurvedic Medicine: The oldest recorded healing tradition; looks at body type, personality characteristics, and five universal elements.

Caduceus: An ancient hermetic symbol of human body, mind, and spirit.

Communication Powers: The three distinct personality aspects that govern human communication.

East-West Current: The energetic pattern of the Environment Power; resembles a spring or coiling vine.

Emotional Powers: The three distinct personality aspects that oversee emotional engagement in life.

Environment Power: The first aspect of personality; governs the nervous system; established at birth.

Expression Power: The second aspect of personality; governs the glandular system; established at three months old.

Helical Energy Current: The energy pattern of Life Force Power; resembles the DNA helix.

Hologram: A three-dimensional frequency pattern created by laser light.

Intention Power: The fifth aspect of personality; governs body tissues; established at one year old.

Inner Vibrancy Signature: The three inner aspects of personality: Emotional, Communication, and Mental Powers.

Intimacy Power: The third aspect of personality; governs the organ system; established at six months old.

Life Force Power: The fourth aspect of personality; governs the joints and senses; established at nine months old.

Longitudinal Current: The energetic pattern of the Intimacy Power; flows up and down the body through the fingers and toes.

Mental Powers: The three distinct personality aspects that oversee cognitive abilities and mental processing.

Polarity Therapy: The therapeutic system developed by Dr. Randolph Stone that balances body energy flow.

Primary Vibrancy Signature: The first five Vibrancy Powers of personality; established in the first year of life.

Radiant Energy Current: The energy pattern of the Intention Power; radiates like a dandelion going to seed.

Shadow of Vibrancy Power: Expressing the opposite of the light-filled qualities and living in the darkness.

Slinky Current: The energy pattern of the Environment Power; also named East-West Current.

Spiral Energy Current: The energy pattern of the Expression Power; spirals like tree rings.

Universal Elements: The foundation of Ayurvedic medicine: earth, water, fire, air, and space/ether.

Vibrancy Colors: Each Vibrancy Power has specific light frequencies that have a colorful name.

Vibrancy Essences: Fifty-two unique formulations derived from specific flowers, gems, and light-infused water.

Vibrancy Healing: Specific guidance for balancing the root cause(s) of any stress pattern in the body, mind, and spirit.

Vibrancy Path: Developed by Jamie Champion, this supports understanding and healing a person's Vibrancy Signature uniqueness.

Vibrancy Powers: Fifty-two distinct Powers of humanity correlated to psychological and physiological vitality.

Vibrancy Signature: The one-of-a-kind energetic blueprint of each person's personality.

Vibrancy Signature Aspect: Five distinct personality areas: environment, expression, intimacy, life force, and intention.

Wireless Anatomy: A term coined by Dr. Randolph Stone to describe energy patterns within the human body.

APPENDIX I

The Complete List of 52 Powers

The Vibrancy Signature

VIBRANCY POWER	VIBRANCY COLOR	HEALTHY CHARACTERISTICS
Abundance	Gold	generous, prosperous, change-agent, needs positions of authority and respect
Accountability	Plum	accomplishment-oriented, task-focused manager, list maker, trustworthy
Aliveness	Lapis Blue	dynamically expressive, charismatic, performance-oriented, enlivening
Altruism	Blue Topaz	deeply values life, purpose-driven, committed to humanitarian causes, activist
Authenticity	Lavender	keeps it real, stays true to self, unconventional, values freedom, free spirit
Balance	White Gold	prioritizes life balance, spiritually-minded, supports living higher values
Brilliance	Orange Topaz	innovative, problem-solver, out-of-the-box thinker, heightened mental awareness
Commitment	Blue	devoted, deep feeling, emotionally expressive, supports personal transformation
Compassion	White	communes on a feeling level, emotionally comforting, good listener, empathetic
Concentration	Green	smart, logical, efficient, good memory, level-headed, tech and data-oriented
Confidence	Magenta	can-do attitude, needs goals, thrives on pressure, creative, encouraging of others
Connection	Indigo Topaz	inclusive, bridge-builder, promotes cooperation, appreciates diversity, diplomatic
Conviction	Lime	verbally expressive, articulate, persuasive, thrives on intelligent discussion
Coordination	Turquoise	graceful, stylish, creative designer, natural multi-tasker, juggles life smoothly

The Complete List of 52 Powers

SHADOW CONTRACTED	SHADOW EXCESSIVE	ELEMENT
financially challenged, resists change, authority issues	greedy, domineering, demanding, power-hungry	space
procrastinates, breaks agreements, makes excuses	micro-manages, sets unrealistic deadlines, inflexible	water
low vitality, shy, shut down, performance anxiety	craves attention, uses charisma to manipulate	water
self-absorbed, depressed, anxious, addictive behaviors	consumed by a cause, self-sacrificing, martyrdom	water
fake, follower, craves acceptance, duty-bound	rebellious, no impulse control, self-destructive	fire
materialistic, confused about priorities, workaholism	proselytizer, judgmental, obsessive-compulsive	water
hoarder, caught in problems, mentally dull	spacey, scattered, delusional, paranoid	water
can't commit, unfaithful, stuck in trauma	cathartic, "dumping" emotions, endures abuse	water
denies feelings, unsympathetic, emotionally cold	over-processes feelings, drowns in emotions	space
slow to learn, forgetful, illogical, irrational	overly analytical, intellectually egoic, unfeeling	air
low self-esteem, no goals, folds under pressure	pushy, bragging, critical, creates undue pressure	space
unsocial, prejudiced, excluding or discounting people	people-pleasing, loses self in a group	fire
tongue-tied, inarticulate, no voice or opinion	always talking, unyielding, loud, arguing	fire
awkward, clumsy, slovenly, unable to manage life	pretentious, scattered from multitasking	space

The Vibrancy Signature

VIBRANCY POWER	VIBRANCY COLOR	HEALTHY CHARACTERISTICS
Courage	Mango	adventurous, faces fears, good at calculating risk, responsive in emergencies
Creativity	Purple Gold	celebrates uniqueness, sees everyone's innate beauty, nurtures elevated artistry
Discernment	Green Gold	unbiased, seeks peaceful resolutions, good at sorting fact from fiction
Empowerment	Ultraviolet	assertive, not easily intimidated, driven to move dreams and visions forward
Energizing	Saffron	highly focused and launches into action when challenged, needs intense exercise
Enthusiasm	Blue Green	excited about life, animated, powerful influencer, health and nutrition advocate
Fun	Yellow	playful, joyful spirit, artsy, crafty, life of the party, can turn anything into a game
Growing	Red Gold	embraces self-discovery, transforms stagnation into new growth, always evolving
Guidance	Violet Gold	lives by principles, makes good choices, promotes taking responsibility for actions
Healing	Crystal	committed to healthy and sustainable results, thrives on clarity, feels subtle energy
Honesty	Red	hard working, values truth, seeks justice, needs strength-building activities
Hope	Violet	idealistic, sees possibilities, offers uplifting perspective, shares visionary ideas
Imagination	Yellow Crystal	driven to design a joyful life, imaginative, turns playful ideas into creative realities
Inspiration	Apricot	full of wonder, lives an inspired life, highly perceptive, creatively embellishes
Integrity	Red Topaz	has high standards, values boundaries and clear agreements, naturally athletic

The Complete List of 52 Powers

SHADOW CONTRACTED	SHADOW EXCESSIVE	ELEMENT
overly cautious, fearful, freezes up, gives up on living	adrenaline addict, fighting, attracts challenges	fire
creatively blocked, feels unexceptional, minimizes self	flamboyant, self-inflated, diva, tortured artist	water
irrational, biased, ignores or creates conflict	over-deliberates, fault-finding, judging others	space
intimidated, passive-aggressive, low motivation	intimidating, hostile, aggressive	fire
sluggish, unfocused, can't handle intensity	never rests, goes to extremes, exhausted	fire
melancholy, lacks affect, junk-food addict	hyper, frenetic, overly dramatic, rigid with health	air
joyless, boring, party-pooper, overworked	irresponsible, party-animal, quits when it's no fun	fire
unwilling to evolve, stuck in unhealthy patterns	never satisfied with self, destructive	space
unethical, ignores consequences, irresponsible	self-righteous, imposes their ideals on others	earth
ungrounded, unclear, unhealthy, numb to subtlety	hyper-sensitive to energy, rigid health guidelines	earth
lying, cheating, stealing, unethical, weak, lazy	ruthlessly truthful, righteous indignation, enforcer	earth
no vision for future, hopeless, fatalistic, distracted	unrealistic, denies present reality, lost in dreams	air
victimhood, complains, no creative ingenuity	impractical, over-designs, lives in a fantasy world	fire
dull, bored, stuck in monotonous routine, imperceptive	sensory overwhelm, never satisfied, perfectionism	fire
can't set boundaries, breaks rules, avoids exercise	rigid boundaries, enforces rules, exercise addict	air

The Vibrancy Signature

VIBRANCY POWER	VIBRANCY COLOR	HEALTHY CHARACTERISTICS
Intuition	Indigo	spontaneous knowing, needs to trust instincts, thrives with nature and animals
Laughter	Lemon	funny, quick-witted, reframes difficulties with humorous perspective
Leadership	Nectarine	has natural business savvy, provides structure for success, values timeliness
Light Heartedness	Yellow Gold	prefers silliness to drama and seriousness, handles life's ups and downs easily
Love	Pink	openhearted, gives love easily, gentle, promotes kindness, likes to give hugs
Manifesting	Violet Crystal	dreams big and believes it's possible, takes action to bring vision into reality
Mindfulness	Silver Gold	spiritually-oriented, attentive, reverent, practices present-moment awareness
Optimism	Mocha Gold	positive mindset, resourceful, self-reliant, practical, methodical problem-solver
Organizing	Orange	devises and maintains systems that keep order, methodical, meticulous, alert
Patience	Blue Gold	even-tempered nature, accepting, nurturing, caring, steady, calming
Persistence	Topaz	establishes habits, reliable, relentless, has an iron will, needs consistent routines
Precision	Emerald	observant, decisive, laser-like accuracy, finds most efficient way to move forward
Prevention	Sea Blue	sensitive, needs to feel safe, proactive, wellness-oriented, safety-minded
Protection	Orange Gold	strategically-minded, advocates for the underdog, safeguards what matters
Relaxation	Mocha	unwinds easily, good at simplifying, keeps life uncomplicated, Zen-like creativity

The Complete List of 52 Powers

SHADOW CONTRACTED	SHADOW EXCESSIVE	ELEMENT
discounts intuition, dislikes animals, avoids nature	lost in intuition, prefers animals over people	air
can't laugh and take a joke, sour attitude about past	sarcastic, ridiculing, irreverent, tasteless humor	air
won't take charge, haphazard, chronically late	controlling, rigid with time, puts profits before people	air
cynical, over-serious, drama magnet, lost in suffering	overly foolish, never serious, inappropriate clowning	fire
heartless, mean-spirited, isolated, feels unlovable	can't deal with world's cruelty, clingy, pushover	water
no aspirations, limiting beliefs, no future plans	self-aggrandizing, over-building, flaunting	space
not present, over multi-tasking, disconnected from spirit	overly ritualistic, disconnected from world	air
pessimistic, negative, dependent, unprepared	blindly optimistic, refusing help, survivalist mindset	earth
disorganized, messy, can't clean up, goes unconscious	needing perfect order, obsessive-compulsive cleaning	earth
impatient, intolerant, reactive, ill-tempered, confronting	enables bad behavior, tolerates mistreatment	water
undisciplined, unable to stick with something, unreliable	inflexible, stubborn, compulsive habits	earth
vague, wordy, indecisive, can't speak up, inefficient	hyper-vigilant, abrupt, abrasive, tactless	space
careless, insensitive, risky, rude, reckless, unhealthy	feels unsafe, shy, germ-phobic, hypochondriac	space
feels beaten down by life, can't protect self, chaotic	overprotective, codependent rescuer, combative	fire
uptight, anxious, stressed, makes life overly complicated	lethargic, zoned out, lackluster, inactive	space

The Vibrancy Signature

VIBRANCY POWER	VIBRANCY COLOR	HEALTHY CHARACTERISTICS
Revealing	Ultraviolet White	emotionally fearless, uninhibited, comfortable with sexuality, faces deep issues
Sensuality	Purple	values beauty and artistry, savors nourishing experiences, sensory sensitivity
Sharing	Peach	friendly, talkative, has many resources, communicates helpful advice, forgiving
Stability	Sky Blue	emotionally steady, grounded during change, provides comfort, natural parent
Support	Silver	service-oriented, volunteer spirit, needs to give and receive support equally
Trust	Indigo Gold	values being in the flow, listens to body's messages, connected to nature's rhythms
Understanding	Green Topaz	curious, loves to learn, updates and shares information with others, scholarly
Wisdom	Black Gold	enjoys deep contemplation, needs mental clarity, looks for spiritual meaning

The Complete List of 52 Powers

SHADOW CONTRACTED	SHADOW EXCESSIVE	ELEMENT
inhibited, embarrassed, denies personal issues, panicky	overshares personal issues, exhibitionist, sex addict	fire
can't take in beauty, gives caustic feedback, unromantic	self-indulgent, superficial beauty, romanticizes	water
uncommunicative, unhelpful, withholding, unforgiving	pushy with unsolicited advice, overly-apologetic	earth
unstable, needy, emotional roller-coaster, neglectful	smothering, spoiling, lets others take advantage	earth
feels unsupported, can't receive, unavailable	no self-care, burned out from overgiving	water
second-guesses, feels out of the flow, mistrusts nature	trusts blindly, ignores facts, superstitious	air
disinterested, incurious, indifferent, feels stupid	overloads with information, questions invasively	fire
superficial, mentally confused, spiritually numb	gets lost in inner world, overcomplicates	fire

ACKNOWLEDGMENTS

First, I would like to acknowledge my teachers, mentors, and inspirational catalysts for the support and encouragement you've given me on my own personal Vibrancy Path journey.

Much gratitude to Max Heirich, who sparked and opened my mind with his enlightening Western versus Non-Western Medicine course at the University of Michigan. Thanks also to my friend, healer, and brilliant catalyst Bill Chilton, who shed light on my creative process and healing journey. I wish to thank my polarity therapy teachers, Dr. James Said and Dr. Pierre Pannetier, along with many others in the polarity community who gave me the framework that Vibrancy Path is based on.

I am so grateful to all my natural healing and nutrition teachers and mentors. Starting with Ki, a medicine woman from Michigan, who mentored me in designing an independent study in Advanced Botany. Also Dr. Ann Wigmore, for her playful wisdom, passion, and mentorship as developer of the Hippocrates raw food nutrition system. Thanks to all the expert guests on my radio show *Ask the Nutritionist*, including Dr. John Ott.

I offer my heartfelt appreciation to my Science of the Soul teachers—Charan Singh, Gurinder Dhillon, and Jasdeep Gill—who have shed light on the purpose of our human birth. They set an example of living life with love as our guiding principle. I am forever grateful for their guidance and wisdom in answering my deepest questions and concerns. One of their directives to me was to make sure that the Vibrancy Path was grounded and based on scientific principles, which has been my core mission in offering this work to the world.

Again, much love and appreciation to my wife Chaya, my life and creative partner who enhances every idea I have with her insight, clarity, and inspirational refinement.

Lastly, my gratitude to the thousands of people around the world who have been open to learning about their Vibrancy Signatures and allowing me to support them in following their own Vibrancy Path journeys. Today, my Vibrancy Path team of John Drennan, Brooke Haynes, and Lisa Drennan, and my long-term colleague Sallie Justice, are helping me bring this system of knowing your true self to the world. Currently, this venture of book writing is made possible by the inspired guidance of Modern Wisdom Press, headed up by Catherine Gregory, Nathan Joblin, and their talented team.

A SPECIAL GIFT FOR YOU

Thank you for joining me on this journey! As a token of appreciation, enjoy a free month of participation in the Vibrancy Path Community, our inspiring online platform where we share monthly events, expert guidance, and soul-nourishing support to help you live your most vibrant, healthy, and authentic life. Claim your gift at www.vibrancypath.com/community and use the discount code **VPBook**. You may also access it via this QR code: